Musician's Survival Guide

to life on the road

＊

Stella Hemmings

PC Publishing

PC Publishing
Export House
130 Vale Road
Kent TN9 1SP
UK

Tel 01732 770893
Fax 01732 770268
email info@pc-pubs.demon.co.uk
website http://www.pc-pubs.demon.co.uk

First published 1998
© PC Publishing

ISBN 1 870775 54 6

British Library Cataloguing in Publication Data
A catalogue record for this book is available from the British Library

Printed in Great Britain by Bell & Bain, Glasgow

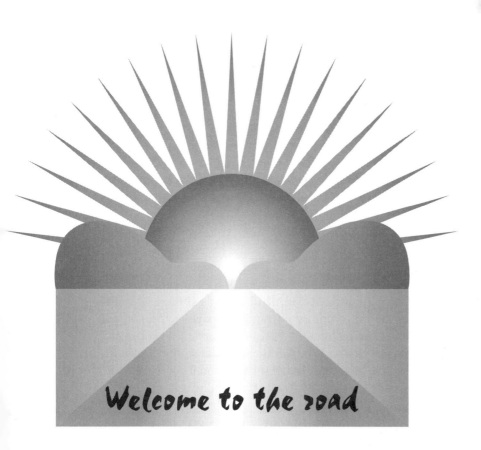

Welcome to the road

T alk to musicians about their experiences on the road and you are unlikely to receive an indifferent response. Some will voice their opinion in a rapturous 'Yeah, brilliant. Love it. Can't wait for the next tour.' Others will be less passionate about the experience and will offer any one of a hundred tales of van breakdowns, missed ferries, lost passports, bad hotels and worse sound systems, as an explanation. The road can indeed be a harsh mistress. Why else would it be the subject of thousands of popular songs?

The road is also a place of opportunity. Few musicians gain recognition playing in their local pub or town hall anymore. It's touring which wins new fans, sells more records/CDs, and which can open the door to interest from record company executives, managers and agents, more than any other promotional tool. And if that were not enough there is nothing like the regimen of gigging six nights a week to enable musicians to hone their craft. Inevitably these are all elements which have the ability to steer the musician towards bigger and better dressing rooms.

Whether you are a seasoned 'road' musician or about to embark on your first tour, this book is designed to place all the information you need at your fingertips. Whether your guitar was crushed in transit, the contract you've been sent looks as though it was translated from Swahili, the House PA seems to have been put together by a deaf sadist, or the immigration officer in front of you doesn't like musicians (no immigration officer likes musicians) this book is designed to help you overcome these difficulties.

The road you are on has been travelled before by many famous and successful artists and musicians, each with their own story to tell. Some of their experiences and adventures are included in these pages along with their own personal, invaluable survival guide advice. Hopefully their experiences and the information contained within these pages will help guide you to a safe, life enriching, and profitable, road loving career.

Special thanks go to all the musicians who contributed anecdotes and who shared their personal experiences of life on the road. They are Benny Rietveld, Billy Hulting, Bobby Messano, Carol Kaye, Dawayne Bailey, Gene Williams, Julie Homi, Kevin Dukes, Martin Jenner, Steve Howard, Susie Davis and Tim Scott.

Happy gigging!

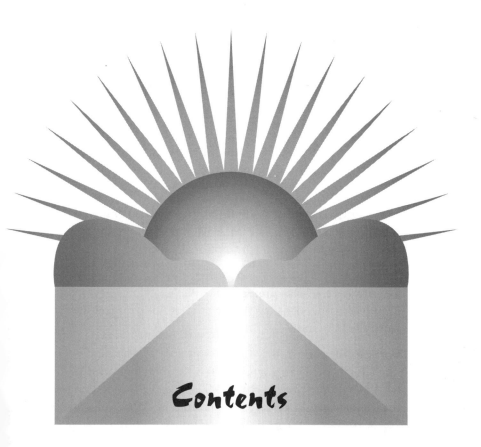

Contents

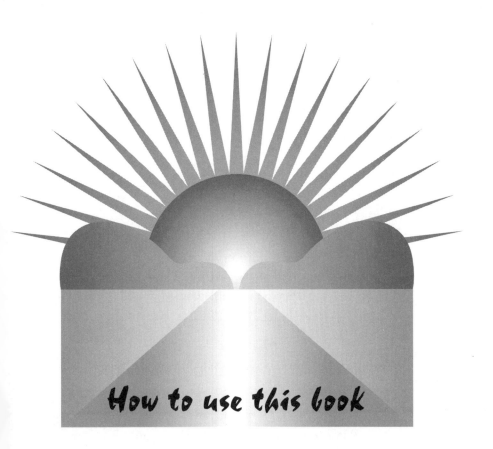

How to use this book

As every gigging performer knows, the old saying 'whatever can go wrong will go wrong, and usually at the most inopportune moment,' was most likely originated by a musician on tour. Some drunken punter had probably just knocked his guitar off its stand or tipped a pint over his keyboard at the time (the quote is the gist of what he said, of course, as his actual words are unprintable).

Touring is a chaos magnet for bizarre and unusual happenings. Just the suggestion of tour dates is often enough to start previously reliable equipment breaking down (or even worse, developing intermittent faults), band members getting sick, van engines blowing up etc. This survival guide aims to give the sinister forces behind these events a run for their money by creating a step by step guide to making your life on the road as pain free as possible.

If you are looking for an answer to a specific question look for the relevant chapter heading and sub-section. Each chapter is self-contained, and where necessary you will be directed to other pages for additional relevant information.

Musicians' Rules Of The Road

Anything that can go wrong will go wrong.

Anything that can't go wrong will go wrong.

When things go right you won't realise it until they go wrong again.

Nothing happens quickly unless you don't want it to.

The time to be most alarmed is when you think everything is under control.

1
Planning

In an ideal world tour planning would be a leisurely and uncomplicated process. As every musician who has ever toured knows, an ideal world is no place ever listed on a professional musicians' itinerary. It may be that you are filling in for another band (or artist) at short notice, or you may be a musician replacing a band member who has just quit, or fallen ill, but the chances are high that you will not have much time to mull over your options when the call comes. This chapter deals with ways to make your life easier.

Appoint a band leader or spokesperson

Even if you are in the fortunate position of having your own management or representation to look after the paperwork side of pre-tour planning, there is still a degree of legwork you will have to do yourself. Without representation you will have to do it all, but this isn't half as tedious as it sounds. Once the information is gathered it doesn't tend to change much and you can put it to one side and forget about it.

For bands, life can be much easier if one person is elected spokesperson to deal with agents/managers and media etc. Not only does it prevent vital information being lost or forgotten in the 'I thought you were doing that' scenarios that frequently occur between band members, but the additional bonus is that it presents a professional image to agents/managers and makes you the kind of band they love to deal with (a point not to be underestimated and one covered in greater detail in Chapter 5).

Who should you pick?

This job often naturally falls to the person who looks after the band's gig diary but it could be any member.

If you are a solo musician the task is yours, of course (but you can take comfort in being the envy of bands throughout the universe for having the sole ego to deal with).

First things first

Whether the tour or engagement is taking place at home or abroad it should be covered by a written contract. Unless you are familiar with contract law it would be unwise to sign anything without first having it vetted by an informed source. It is sad but true that the music industry is full of people who will gladly take advantage of your inexperience and that even the most straightforward looking contracts may have hidden pitfalls. The Musician's Union offers free contract advice to its members (it also offers other services such as subsidised equipment insurance, public liability insurance, and other bonuses covered in greater detail in Chapter 2). Non MU members should seek the advice of a lawyer who specialises in the music business. A lawyer is likely to be more expensive but you may qualify for legal aid or 'Green Form' work (see Chapter 2 for more information on contracts and legal advice).

What your tour manager/agent/band leader will need from you

If you are touring overseas the first thing you will need are photocopies of each tour members' passports. (Passport information is covered in depth in Chapter 11, this is just a quick look at the information you will need to deliver.) Some agents ask for photocopies of the first seven pages even if they are blank (welcome to the strange world of bureaucracy), but most require a copy of just the page with the personal information on, i.e. name, date and place of birth, where the passport was issued, when it expires etc.

If at this stage you don't have a passport you are rightly entitled to panic because trying to get a passport application processed at speed can be stressful (see Chapter 11, Passports and visas).

Your band leader/ agent/ tour manager will also need a list of the equipment you intend taking with you, for three reasons:

1 Carnet (pronounced 'carnay') or manifest documentation. These documents helps to expedite customs clearance of your equipment at home and abroad (more on carnets and manifests later in this chapter).
2 For insurance purposes you will need to supply the serial numbers of each piece of equipment, copies of purchase receipts, and an estimate of current or replacement value (see Chapter 3, Insurance).
3 For transportation or freight forwarding your band leader will also need a note of the dimensions and weight of the equipment.

> **✳ ✳ ✳**
> **✳ TIP ✳**
> If your passport is close to expiring (within six to nine months) apply for a new one. Many countries will not let you enter unless you have at least six months life left on it, even if you are intending only a short visit. Also, if you enter the country a borderline case and find that after fulfilling your engagement you or your band are invited to add extra dates (these things do happen), you might not be able to because your passport is too close to expiry. Can't stress enough how unpopular that makes you with other band members. It's also disappointing for you to miss extra opportunities.

Q & A with Billy Hulting

Q What information does the artist's manager/tour manager want from you?

A Social Security numbers, passport information, a list of cases you will be bringing. You only need a detailed list of your gear (serial numbers and all) if you are traveling out of the country for the manifest to show to customs. You also need to let them know about any special needs, non-smoking rooms, for example. Also, any special diet requirements for when you are getting a catered meal. On Lou's gig, Curtis (bass player) and I have a vegan diet – Lou's tour manager, John Molinare, had us print up a vegan menu for him to fax ahead to the promoter for the gigs which provide dinner. He also sent a list of our frequent flyer numbers, preferred seats, and special meal requests to the travel agent so they can enter the info in while booking our flights – what a guy!

Billy Hulting, percussionist with: Lou Rawls, Natalie Cole, Barry Manilow, Maynard Ferguson.

Q & A with Julie Homi

Q What information does the artist's manager/tour manager want from you?

A They always want basic data, such as address, phone number and social security number. As a registered alien living in the US, I have to provide a copy of my green card. If the tour is going abroad, they will ask for passport information. Tour managers often ask my plane seating preference, and if I require a non-smoking hotel room. They may ask what I like to drink onstage and backstage.

One thoughtful tour manager even asked me if I had a bunk preference on the bus. They always ask for an equipment list, which is usually finalized during rehearsal. Sometimes, they ask for a bio and/or a photo to put in the program.
Julie Homi, keyboard player with: Peter Cetera, Tracy Chapman, Yanni, Martin Page.

What your tour manager will need from you
Checklist

✔ Photocopy of your passport details

✔ Social Security, or National Insurance Number

✔ Your address

✔ Bank account details

✔ List of the equipment you are taking on tour

✔ Serial numbers of equipment

✔ Any extra requests such as meal preferences, smoking or non-smoking rooms etc.

Carnet questions and answers

What is a carnet?

For a musician a carnet (or manifest) is an itemised list of every piece of professional equipment you are temporarily transporting into or through a country overseas, for the purpose of performance. The carnet enables you to cross borders without having to pay customs duties and taxes on your gear in the country you are entering, and saves you from having to complete lengthy customs documentation.

What is the purpose of the carnet?

Economic security for the country or countries you are passing through or performing in. Carnet, or manifest documentation is designed to prevent people from selling goods in foreign countries without them paying the required customs and excise duty. It goes without saying therefore that every piece of equipment which enters a country should also leave the country. Anything missing will be liable for customs duty, tax or a penalty.

Do I have to have one?

It is not always a legal requirement but is usually desirable to have one. Being a carnet holder shows your intent to conform to that country's laws and tends to speed up your processing at customs crossings.

What happens if I travel without a carnet?

As everyone who has passed a customs check point knows, you are just as likely to be waved through without anyone wanting to even glance at your paperwork as you are to be stopped and given the third degree. Even if you are stopped much of what happens will have more to do with how you react to the customs officer's questions and what kind of day he or she is having than any paperwork you may or may not be holding. Unless you regard customs baiting a sport, it's more helpful to imagine that every time a customs officer leaves his/her cubicle they are singing Snap's 'I've Got The Power,' to themselves and recognise that yes, they have. If they wish they are perfectly entitled to ask you to remove every single piece of equipment from your vehicle for cross-checking against your documentation. Not only is this a major irritation but it can also delay you for hours.

Warning: If you don't have a carnet, Customs may impound your equipment or require you to hand over a substantial financial bond as assurity that all of your equipment will leave with you.

What if any of the gear listed on the carnet or manifest is stolen?

Any goods which don't make the return journey home automatically become liable for customs duty even if they are stolen.

What if the carnet document itself is lost or stolen?

You will have a tedious day. In this event you should notify the local police and your nearest customs office and obtain a statement from them. If you keep a note of your carnet/manifest number the Chamber of Commerce or your Customs and Excise department will be able to issue a Carnet Duplicate for which they will charge you the carnet fee again. If the carnet is recovered you can return the duplicate and be reimbursed. If the carnet is not recovered you will have to wait for it to expire plus six months when as long as no one else has used it the carnet will be cleared and your deposit returned.

How do I apply for a carnet?
Contact either your Chamber of Commerce, Customs and Excise, or department of trade and industry. They will be able to forward to you the necessary forms and most will also be able to provide you with a booklet explaining in detail how the system works.

How much does a carnet cost?
Currently around £170 ($280) plus a returnable bond which will be a percentage of the equipment value.

Do I have to apply for a carnet myself?
Not necessarily. If you are being hired to join a tour your tour manager will take care of the carnet or manifest. Even if you are arranging your own travel, if you don't want to be bothered with the carnet yourself there are companies who offer preparation and carnet management services on your behalf - for a fee. These can be found listed in musician resource guides such as as the Music Week Directory, or Recording Industry Sourcebook, or similar.

If I am from an EEC country do I need a carnet for travelling within the EEC community?
No, members of the European community need only contact their local Customs & Excise office and ask for form C&E 1246 Returned Goods Release. It is a form which asks you to list all of the equipment you are carrying - much the same as a carnet - and serving the same purpose. This form is available free of charge.

Before you pack

Check out the tools of your trade.
This is the time to make sure all your gear is in good, roadworthy, working order. If you have been putting up with strange hums, clicks, dodgy cables and connections recently put up with them no more. These problems are far easier to eradicate at home than they are on tour.

Similarly, check over all of your mains leads. Any cable which has nicks in the insulating sleeve or just generally looks worn and tatty should be replaced.

TIP

If there is a possibility you will make multiple visits abroad ask for additional vouchers at the time of applying for your carnet (the Chamber of Commerce will supply you with up to 90 if requested). The carnet is valid for twelve months and as long as your equipment list remains the same you will be able to travel on the same documents and avoid having to reapply and pay additional carnet fees.

❛I'm always wireless. I haven't had a corded guitar system for 15 years. I've had a couple of really bad incidents of pseudo electrocution. I was knocked out once on stage by a bad ground, and I ended up on the floor completely knocked out with my guitar on top of me, with my gums bleeding. 'Cos someone cut a ground someplace and no one realised it. All I saw was a big spark and that was the end of time for a few minutes.❜ *Bobby Messano (guitar: Steve Winwood, Robin Beck).*

The more you travel the more you become aware that international safety standards are not universally recognised and that some territories consider them unnecessarily stringent. Some countries appear cavalier, particularly when it comes to electric shock avoidance.

❛Setting up for a gig during a Middle East tour one of the crew noticed that several of the mains cables had wads of snazzy coloured insulating tape wound around them. After taking a closer look we found that not only was the tape covering exposed wires it was also all that was holding the cable together. We showed this to the club's resident engineer but he didn't see it as any kind of problem and swore that it was quite safe. It wasn't until we suggested he held the taped connection with both hands while standing in a bucket of water that he decided to replace the cables with less colourful ones.❜ *(Sound engineer for The Commitments).*

Not all electrical accidents happen with so obvious a potential cause. The moral of this story, and others like it is that, if you don't already possess one, buy a circuit breaker or Residual Current Detector (RCD). These are available in any electrical store and are designed to cut off the mains supply before you receive an electric shock. They don't come with a 100% guarantee but at least they are an effective first line of defense.

✳ ✳ ✳
✳ **TIP** ✳

Don't forget to include your mains boards in your maintenance check. Screws loosen over time due to the vibratory effect of mains current and need to be re-tightened. The only thing worse than having your equipment go dead on stage is having yourself go dead due to a poor earth connection. Some might argue there is a publicity advantage to be gained from such an incident but you won't be around to reap the benefit.

✳ ✳ ✳
✳ **TIP** ✳

Buy a circuit breaker or residual current detector (RCD)

Q & A with Martin Jenner

Q What has been the most alarming technical problem you have experienced on stage?

A In Germany in the early 60's being constantly thrown across stage by 'stray' current going through the mike to the guitar via me. the incredibly fast 'cut-out' safety devices of today were not available then. Scary moments!' *Martin Jenner (guitar: Cliff Richard, Everly Brothers).*

If you are touring with computer equipment you will almost certainly need a mains filter or mains current smoother to protect it from damaging power surges or mains spikes (available from computer and most electrical stores).

Medical insurance
Travelling abroad always presents the possibility of illness or accidents no matter how careful you are. With emergency medical care ranging from costly to exorbitant, depending on which part of the world you are in, you should ensure that you are covered for any medical treatment you may require. While travelling within EEC countries citizens of member countries can take advantage of the reciprocal medical service arrangements between EEC countries. Before you leave visit your local DHSS office and pick up a form E111 for each crew/band member (see Chapter 3 for more information and for travel to non EEC countries).

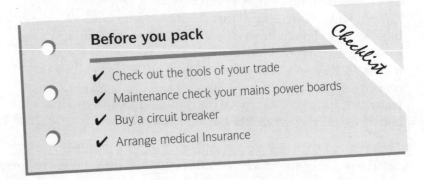

Before you pack

Checklist

✔ Check out the tools of your trade

✔ Maintenance check your mains power boards

✔ Buy a circuit breaker

✔ Arrange medical Insurance

Making the most of your itinerary

The only time you will realise your agent/promoter/manager has a sense of humour is when you read your itinerary. Unless you are heading for a residency gig you are likely to be enrolling on a schedule which offers a different venue, and perhaps even a different country, every night. Time can get tight, especially when such things as traffic delays, bad weather and vehicle breakdowns enter the equation. Unless you are psychic there is not a lot you can do about those other than aim for prevention, but there are ways you can help yourself should such events occur.

Allow extra time to get to your destination. An obvious one really but also one of the most important. Underestimating by even half an hour might make the difference between getting a decent soundcheck in or not getting one at all. Giving yourself a buffer zone helps to limit the effect of delays.

❛ I've been on some pretty challenging tours. A low budget mini van tour of Europe with a road manager who kept underestimating the length of our daily drives was a grind. He had us traveling for 5, 6, 7 hours a day, arrive at the gig just in time for soundcheck, do the performance, retire to a hotel to sleep and get up to do it again the next day. Needless to say everyone was exhausted and sick by its end and if you think we were tired you should have seen the poor crew. ❜ Susie Davis (keyboards: Billy Idol, Sinead O'connor, Van Morrison).

Have your equipment clearly marked so that you or your roadies will immediately know what it is and where it goes. It saves spending a significant amount of time having to delve inside the transport cases to identify the contents and then moving it around to its correct location. It also helps your road crew to devise a packing/unpacking strategy.

Be well rehearsed so that even if you are arriving at a venue later than scheduled you are ready to perform.

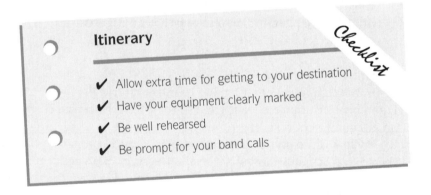

Itinerary   *Checklist*

✔ Allow extra time for getting to your destination
✔ Have your equipment clearly marked
✔ Be well rehearsed
✔ Be prompt for your band calls

Getting there: the question of transport

If you are about to join a tour where all you have to do is arrive at the pick-up point, get on the tour bus, and sit back and enjoy the rest of the journey, then you were indeed born under a good moon. Good luck and hard work make those things happen, but it's quite likely that before you reach that stage your touring experience will involve your being one of half a dozen or so band members crammed into a VW bus (or similar), squeezed uncomfortably between instrument cases for interminable periods of time (and people think a musician's life is glamorous).

If your transport is your own, or the joint property of the band, there are some other avenues worth considering.

1 Hiring a self-drive van or minibus
2 Hiring a tour bus plus a driver
3 AA, RAC, Green Flag or similar membership

Hiring a self-drive van or minibus
It will add to the expense of travelling but has some distinct advantages.

* Subject to your budget you'll be able to choose a vehicle large enough to comfortably accommodate the band and equipment.
* The vehicle will probably be a newer model than your own and potentially more reliable.
* Depending on your hire agreement, if you break down your hire company will not only retrieve your vehicle but will replace it with another. In one fell swoop this saves you the trouble (should your own vehicle break down) of having to get it towed off the road, finding a mechanic/garage to carry out the necessary repairs, and facing uncertain delays.
* Transport hire is a tax deductible expense, and also one that with forward planning, you may be able to negotiate into your contract in advance.

Warning
Insurance companies don't tend to be musician friendly. Equipment insurance is loaded and so too is vehicle insurance. In an attempt to cut costs there may be a temptation to forget to tell the hire company (or your personal insurance company) that the driver/occupants are musicians. In the event of an accident this could get tricky. If the Insurance company discovers that you didn't disclose the nature of your occupation they are within their rights to reject your claim and leave you to face the consequences - a hefty bill proportional to the severity of the accident (more on vehicle insurance later in this chapter).

Hiring a tour bus plus a driver
This has the same benefits as hiring without but also offers the added bonus of having an experienced driver to get you to your destination. The good news is that whatever fee you pay it will be all inclusive. The bad news is that the cost is likely to mean this option is only available to bands who have record company support.

Hiring a sleeper coach

This option is particularly useful when there are substantial distances to cover between gigs but again, due to the cost, is most often only available to established bands/artists who are signed to record labels.

> ❜Roxy Music used to tour in an old army ambulance which wasn't big enough to carry the whole band. We couldn't get Brian Eno into the ambulance, so we had to slide Eno in horizontally, between the equipment and the ceiling. ❜ *Bryan Ferry talking to Alan Grice (Encore Magazine).*

What can I expect to pay for transport hire?

The cost of hiring vehicles varies so much from region to region that your best bet is to shop around in your local neighbourhood for your own best deal. The Yellow Pages of your telephone directory will be a good place to start. Also, look in any musician's or music industry resource guide (such as the Music Week Directory or Recording Industry Sourcebook) and look under the Vehicle Hire, or Tour Services section for specialist vehicle hire.

Price guidelines

A self-drive twelve seater Volkswagen plus driver can be hired from around £175 ($250 a day). A sleeper coach plus driver(s) will cost approximately £300 ($450) per day.

AA, RAC, Green Flag or similar membership

If you take your own vehicle on tour you will find most motoring organisations worth the cost of membership. They offer comprehensive packages, for both home and abroad, which go beyond vehicle breakdown. Their services become particularly beneficial when driving overseas, especially when you can receive cover which includes emergency assistance or towage, vehicle recovery, vehicle hire if your own is unusable, payment for accommodation if you have to wait for repairs etc. You'll find your nearest representative in your local telephone directory.

Questions vehicle insurance companies ask musicians and why

What type of musician are you, classical or popular?

It can't be avoided. Orchestral or classical musicians are expected to be more sedate than their popular music counterparts, and therefore deemed less of a risk.

Are you freelance or employed?

This is to determine whether you will be using your vehicle predominantly for business use or pleasure.

What type of instrument do you pay?

Once more a factor to determine how great a risk you are likely to be. A lead guitarist will be loaded more than someone who plays the oboe. - Sadly, another painful stereotype but probably one which is well deserved.

What type of venues do you play?

You are deemed a greater risk if you appear at night clubs and pubs than if you play in concert halls. The presence of alcohol is a contributing factor here. Even if you yourself are tee-total your vehicle will be parked in the vicinity of other vehicles driven by owners who are not.

Have you appeared on TV or radio?

A higher profile may mean your vehicle will be the target of vandalism or suffer at the hands of over enthusiastic fans (or tough critics) making you a riskier liability.

Do you have a recording contract?

If you do Insurance companies expect you to have a higher public profile than the average musician. They also expect that in the event of an accident in which an accompanying passenger gets hurt, that passenger is going to be more likely to sue you.

Some insurance companies say that they do not discriminate against musicians and that the only question they will ask is whether you use your vehicle for business as well as non-business use. After a few phone calls you may discover they do not discriminate because all of their insurance policies are loaded. It's worthwhile spending some time shopping around for the best deal even if you have to face twenty questions.

Driving abroad

If you elect the self-drive option there are several things you will need to make yourself aware of.

Your driving licence

First you will need to know what kind of driving license you need to hold. Most countries allow visiting drivers to do so as long as they hold a full licence in their home country, Drivers with only a provisional licence or learner permit are not eligible to drive overseas, but some countries require drivers to hold an International driving licence. To find out what the requirements are for the countries you are visiting contact the relevant tourist information service.

Green cards and insurance

Besides your driving licence a Green Card or other insurance documents are essential. Most motoring associations will be able to advise their members on what degree of cover is appropriate.

Safety rules and regulations

Not all countries have the same rules and regulations when it comes to road safety so it is worth double checking. For most countries the carrying of warning triangles is compulsory, as is wearing seat-belts in both the front and rear seats of the vehicle.

Speed limits

Make yourself aware of the speed restrictions for motorways, dual carriageways, single lane roads and built-up areas. Many countries impose on the spot fines for drivers caught speeding.

Unexpected hazards

Some overseas driving can expose the driver to hazards previously never encountered while driving in their home territory. In Scandinavia, for example, elk or reindeer are prone to wander onto roads without warning. Local drivers know to exercise caution but visitors who are unprepared can easily find themselves off the road, or worse, in collision with one of these enormous animals. Before leaving find out what local hazards may exist in the areas you will be travelling through.

Special considerations

Check if there are any additional driving or highway code laws you are not familiar with. Sweden, for instance, requires vehicles to be driven with headlights on day and night.

Drink driving

Drinking and driving laws vary from region to region. In some countries you will not be able to have even one beer without pushing yourself over the limit. The regions with the strictest laws usually also have the severest penalties. Drivers who drink can expect to lose their licence, face a fine and quite possibly a prison sentence.

Finding accommodation

If you are going to have to find your own accommodation while you are travelling it is well worth investing in a Rough Guide, Lonely Planet or Fodor Guide book or similar for the region you will be visiting. Besides listing addresses and telephone numbers for hotels and guest houses etc., these books also give you an indication of how much you will need to pay, and list accommodations for every budget.

Driving abroad   *Checklist*

✔ Check what type of driving licence is required for the country or countries you will be visiting (i.e. Full or International).

✔ Insurance

✔ Safety rules and regulations

✔ Speed limits

✔ Unexpected hazards

✔ Special considerations

✔ Drink driving restrictions

✔ Accommodation information

2
Contracts

* Do you need one?
* What should be in the contract
* Payment options
* What shouldn't be in the contract
* Technical riders
* Who should draw up the contract
* Contracts with agents
* Legal advice
* Broken contracts
* Contracts between band members
* Musician's unions

W hether the tour or engagement is taking place at home or abroad one of the first things you will need to do will be to discuss the terms and conditions of your contract.

Do I need a contract?

With an agent or venue? Yes, absolutely. Despite weaknesses in some country's legal systems which can make it difficult to recover payment from someone who is reluctant to honour your agreement (which we will go into further later in the chapter), you are still better off with a contract than without for two reasons:

1   A written agreement offers you at least some degree of legal protection, and
2   Issuing or asking for a contract proves that you or your band are experienced professionals who expect to be taken seriously.

The relationship between a musician and the contract can be likened to that of Linus and his security blanket in the Peanuts cartoons. One without the other in either case will not definitely lead to catastrophe, but both feel distinctly more comfortable knowing they are there. If Linus ever gets run over by a cement truck while clutching his beloved blanket the analogy will still stand though, because, at best, a contract can only hope to limit potential damage. The effectiveness of a contract, however carefully prepared, comes down to how exploitable it is in its interpretation (as George Michael will no doubt testify following his lengthy courtroom battle with Sony) and how far you can afford to go if an agent, venue or promoter doesn't wish to honour the agreement.

What should be in the contract?
That depends on you and your agent/promoter. There is no such thing as a standard contract (apart from your own national labour/Musicians Union standard contract which we'll give you more information on later in this chapter). What appears in a contract depends on each promoter and to what lengths he or she is prepared to go to secure your services. A band or artist with a hit single to their credit will have more say in the content of their agreement than a band just starting out, but whichever you are, at the very least, your contract needs to state how much you will be paid, and in what manner you will receive payment.

Payment options
You might be offered a number of options such as a pre-agreed fixed fee paid to you on the night, or a small fee plus a percentage of door takings, or no fee and the whole door take. The most straightforward of these is obviously a fixed fee, especially if you are a new band or act or are going to be performing outside your normal gig zone in an area which hasn't heard of you. If you are a known band or act with your own following you could easily be better off choosing either of

the latter options although you will probably want to make a provision in the contract whereby you will have your own representative at the door to ensure that there is an accurate door count.

The contract should also determine who it is that is going to pay you, whether it will be the agent, promoter or venue (more on this later).

If the engagement requires extensive travel, especially if you are performing overseas, the contract needs to cover all travel and accommodation expenses. These expenses are most often paid by the promoter or agency hiring you.

What else should be in the contract?
Interestingly (following our reference to circuit breakers in the previous chapter) the British Musician's Union have found it necessary to feature a clause in their contracts which makes the venue liable for providing 'a safe supply of electricity.' Important at the best of times, this is particularly significant for outdoor performances where damp weather can create havoc (see sample contract reproduced overleaf).

If the tour or performance is going to have any part of it filmed or recorded for video, film or TV purposes, the contract should state how much the artist, band or musician will be paid for taking part in the recording.

For performances or tours abroad the contract should specify which currency your fee will be paid in (see Chapter 5: Money).

You should also make sure that your contract is written in your own language or, if not, at least has a translation of it attached. It is surprising how many overseas agents do not offer this service as a matter of course and need to be requested to provide it.

What shouldn't be in the contract?
On the whole bands and artists should not be expected to make any payment for using the venue's own PA or lighting systems. Nor should you be required to pay any portion of the venues publicity costs for promoting your performance. You should also look out for any vague terminology written into the contract such as 'other expenses.' The agent might only intend for this to mean that you will have to pay for your own phone bills, but the term could just as easily be interpreted to mean that you are expected to foot the bill for hiring security. To avoid any nasty surprises make sure that the contract terms are clear and not open to inventive interpretation. There also should not be a

TIP
If you are working with an agent or promoter who is new to you or if the contract covers a number of engagements, it is a good idea to ask for some sort of deposit in advance. New acts will probably find it a struggle securing that kind of arrangement, but at the very least your contract should make sure that you receive payments on specific dates during the trip or tour and not be restricted to a lump sum at the end of the tour.

MUSICIANS UNION STANDARD CONTRACT
For the Engagement of a Band/Group for Casual Engagements

An Agreement made on the .... day of .... 19 ....

between...

of...
(Address)
(hereinafter called the "Engager") of the one part,

and ....

of ....
(Address)
(hereinafter called "the Leader") of the other part.

WITNESSES:

1. The Engager engages the Leader to provide a combination of .... musicians
    (number)
    appearing as ....
    (name of band/group)

    to perform for: *dancing/cabaret accompaniment/stage background music....................................
    * Delete whichever is not applicable
    at ....
    (venue/address)

    on the date(s) and at fee(s) listed below:

2. It is agreed that the inclusive fee for the engagement shall be payable in cash /by cheque *(delete whichever is inapplicable)* on the date of the performance.

Dates	Start	Finish	Fee

3. Performance in addition to that specified in Clause 1 above shall be subject to fees and conditions to be agreed between both parties.

4. It is the responsibility of the Engager to ensure that a piano in good playing condition is provided *(delete if inapplicable)*.

5. It is agreed by both parties to this contract that the equipment and instruments of the musician performing for the engagement are not available for use by other performers or persons except by specific permission of the musician.

6. It is the responsibility of the Engager to take all reasonable steps by way of stipulation in booking providing the venue for the engagement, to ensure a safe supply of electricity.

7. The Engager recognises the Musicians' Union as the sole representative organisation for musicians and strongly recommends all musicians to become or remain members of the Union.

8. This Agreement may not be modified or cancelled except by mutual consent, in writing and signed by both parties.

Signed   ....Engager   Signed   ....Musician

Address ....   Address ....

....

Contract to be signed in duplicate. One copy to be retained by the Engager and one to be retained by the Musician.

clause which allows the agent or promoter to cancel the contract without your agreement.

On the opposite page is the Musician's Union sample contract (reproduced by kind permission of the Musician's Union)

Technical riders

Once the basics of your contract have been negotiated and agreed you might have additional requests you wish to include as a technical rider attached to the contract. Whether your promoter will agree to the rider depends on what it is you ask for, how easy it is for them to fulfill your request, and whether they believe you are worth the extra effort it will entail. Established artists might request a specific sound system or sound, stage or lighting set-up in their rider. They might even specify the companies they wish to be hired to supply the equipment. Other riders might have more personal concerns.

Back in the mid seventies when concerts were big business, name acts were able to make excessive demands. It was common for big stars to request extravagant spreads of food in their dressing room, along with a specified number of crates of their preferred choice of alcoholic beverage. It wasn't just limousine travel that was expected for transporting the band or artist to venues or to their hotel, it had to be a particular vehicle model, most likely fitted out with a detailed list of accessories such as a TV, and a stocked bar. Towards the end of the seventies though as the concert business went into decline and big promotion budgets became a rarity, artists and stars were encouraged to become more moderate with their demands. But despite the changing times if their is something you really need to enable you to put on a great show there's no harm in asking.

Strange but true technical rider extracts

Van Halen in their March 1978 tour requested a bowl of M&Ms be made available to them in their dressing room with the brown ones removed; apparently they were attached to the idea of having someone painstakingly hand sort their M&Ms especially for them.

During his 'Addicted To Love' tour Robert Palmer insisted on a backstage supply of Moet et Chandon.

In April 1988, while Aerosmith (who by now were rejecting the drug and alcohol excesses of their earlier days) toured the US with Guns 'n Roses as supporting act, they insisted on a technical rider in their contract requesting that Guns 'n Roses confine any drug and alcohol activities to their own dressing room.

Who should draw up the contract?

More often than not your promoter or agent will expect you to sign their contract for engagements or tours that they are arranging. When dealing directly with venues and clubs for casual engagements you can offer to issue your own or, if you are a Musician's/Labour Union member, you can issue the appropriate union contract (more on Musicians' Unions at the end of this chapter).

I'm not a regular band member but get hired to join tours as a freelance musician. Do I need a contract?

Many musicians take to the road without having any formal, written agreement, and never experience any problems. As long as money gets paid into your bank account at the specified times there is little cause for concern, but to not have a contract still makes you vulnerable to exploitation. Every musician is better off having some form of written agreement. If those who wish to hire you are reluctant to go to the length of issuing you with a full contract, it is worthwhile trying to at least secure a letter of intent.

Advice clinic with Susie Davis

Q What advice would you give musicians regarding contracts?

A You'd be surprised how many managers will hire you with only a verbal contract, but you can get more easily screwed this way. I have been and so I always try to have a basic contractual agreement with an artist. Salary is usually set on a weekly basis but make sure you discuss and are in agreement on how much money you make for any given working day, in the event that you only work a partial week. Usually the amount is based on your weekly salary divided by seven. You'd be surprised how many times I wasn't paid the correct amount for the number of days I worked and had to call the tour accountants and point it out to them. Also make sure that your employers are in agreement that travel days are working days, even if there is no show.

'If you can establish rates for appearing in videos or on TV in advance that can be helpful. Lots of times you'll be in the middle of a tour and find yourself on a video shoot for your artist's new single and you'll realise that you haven't discussed payment putting you at a distinct disadvantage for negotiating. All musicians should be compensated when they make appearances in video, film or on TV. A video should get you a couple days extra salary, while a full length concert video should pull in around a week's salary. This is just from my experience. I'm sure there are other players making a lot more than me ... there always are.
Susie Davis (keyboards: Billy Idol, Go West, Debbie Harry).

'Only Billy Joel ever offered a contract in all my years of touring and he was very generous. Everyone I've had the pleasure of working with, save one person who will remain nameless because he will probably never tour again, had a very good reputation for the treatment of their band members and all business was done on a handshake agreement.' *Kevin Dukes (Guitar: Peter Cetera, Billy Joel).*

Contracts with agents

Agency contracts tend to fall into two categories. Your agent will either operate as an employment agent where they will issue a contract between the venue and the musicians and charge a commission on the fee involved, or they can issue an employment business contract where the agent buys the band or artist for a set fee and then sells them to a venue for a higher fee.

Employment agent contract

This contract will be between the venue and the band and signed by the venue and band representative. Should there be a problem with non-payment or cancellation of the gig the agent cannot be held responsible. The agent will charge a pre-agreed commission fee which will be a percentage of the band's or artist's fee (usually around 15%). The commission is paid by the musicians. For some countries this agreement will also be subject to tax. In Britain most agents will also charge VAT (value added tax) on top, so, for example, a band earning £400 for a gig where the agent charges 15% plus VAT will have to pay the agent £60 plus £9 VAT (15% of £60) bringing a total of £69. Not a bad income for making a phone call some might say.

As with all contracts there should not be a clause which allows an agent to cancel a contract without the agreement of both the venue and the musicians concerned.

TIP Make sure the contract states whether the fee quoted by the agent is before or after their commission has been deducted. The fee stated in a contract between venue and musician should be the fee before deductions.

Employment business contracts

This contract will be between the agent and the band or artist, and will be signed by the agent and band representative or artist. The agent will have a separate contract between him/herself and the venue. Should there be a problem with non-payment or cancellation of the gig it is the agent who is responsible. In this instance the agent is not entitled to charge the musician a commission. They will make their profit by selling your services at a higher price to the venue. How much money the agent earns depends on how much he or she is able to negotiate with the venue. Sadly, the musician has no say when it comes to fixing their selling price. Any additional tax will be charged to the venue. As with all contracts there should not be a clause which allows an agent or the musicians to cancel a contract without the agreement of the agent and musicians concerned.

Do I need legal advice before signing a contract?

Absolutely yes. And not just any legal advice – it needs to be from someone experienced in music business contracts, not your local family lawyer or solicitor, who has probably never seen a music business contract before.

Advice Clinic with Benny Rietveld

Q What advice would you give musicians regarding contracts?

A Read them ... thoroughly. If you can't understand the lingo, get an impartial third party to help you.
Benny Rietveld (bass: Santana, Sheila E, Miles Davis).

Members of Musicians/Labour Unions receive a free contract vetting service as a union benefit. Considering that the cost of becoming a member can be as little as around £50 ($75) per year, and that most legal advice is considerably more expensive, it's worth considering joining your trade union for this alone. Not only will they vet the contract but should you run into problems with a contract they have approved their legal department will act on your behalf and try to help you recover unpaid fees.

Advice clinic with Steve Howard

Q What should be in a contract?

A When you're working for Ray Charles or somebody like that, the job pays what it pays, and that's it. So there's no need for a contract or anything like that – you might have some sort of an agreement that you might sign with them. And the Musicians Union dictates also that, for instance, if you're playing the job live and they want to, say, record the thing, well, you're supposed to get paid extra for that – if they do a live recording. A lot of times artists will try to not pay you for that – I don't think it's necessarily the artists as much

as it is their management. It's a very important thing to get a music attorney, so that you can be covered on all sorts of things like that, so that if they decide to make a film of part of a concert, or press a record, or do a television show, or take a little clip of you playing to make a Pepsi commercial, or whatever – that you can be compensated for that.
Steve Howard (horns: Paul McCartney & Wings, Ray Charles, Albert Collins).

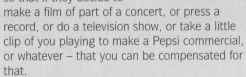

Should you not wish to join a Union you might consider approaching a music business lawyer. Their services are not cheap, but if you are planning a long term career in music this is probably as good a time as any to begin a relationship that will cover all kinds of future contract possibilities. In most territories musicians on a low income can qualify for legal aid.

What do I do if the agent/venue breaks the contract?
The most common ways agents and venues break contracts is either by cancelling the engagement without your permission or by refusing to pay you after completing the gig. If you are a Musicians Union member and the contract in question is one they approved, you can report the problem to your local branch secretary and ask the union to pursue the matter on your behalf. If you are not a member you have to decide how far you want to take it yourself and consider the circumstances surrounding it. If, for example, the gig was cancelled because the venue has been gutted by a fire it's probably not going to be in your best interest to chase them for a settlement. Rescheduling the engagement for a later date would be more diplomatic and most likely to be better received by the people concerned.

Similarly, If the agent is wishing to cancel because of a double booking error on his part, unless this is a common occurrence, instead of causing him or her more grief you could easily be better off accepting an alternative booking as a replacement. Reasonable flexibility should not be underrated but there is a limit. Non-payment after completing a gig should never be tolerated. Even if you happened to be the worst band or artist in the world once you have fulfilled your contractual obligations you should be paid. It's the agent's or venue's responsibility to make sure that you are the type of act they wish to employ before signing a contract.

For a broken contract which covers a number of engagements or a tour, and results in you losing substantial earnings you should consult your lawyer or union regarding legal action.

If the broken engagement is a one off that you wish to pursue yourself, your most likely course of action will be through a Small Claims Court or equivalent system. Be warned though, depending on in which country you are making your claim the results are not always satisfactory. British law, for example, is such that even when ordered to make payment the offending agent or venue can still refuse, and the worse that can happen to them is that their name will be placed in the county court register. All this prevents them from doing is being able to receive credit. In other countries – particularly the US where the claims system is far more aggressive, you are more likely to receive a favourable financial settlement.

It doesn't take long for a musician to discover that a booking agent rarely means what he or she says. The trick is to find out what it is they are *not* saying when they offer you a gig. The following is a Top Ten Guide to favourite agent-speak.

A musician's guide to agent-speak

1 *You're the first band I thought of*
Don't be tempted into feeling flattered, the truth is that no one else will do it.

2 *I've been let down at short notice*
Means that the other band found out more about the gig and refused to do it.

3 *It's a veteran motorcycle rally*
You'll be performing in front of 5000 Hell's Angels.

4 *You have insurance, don't you?*
Because the last band they put in there had their gear trashed.

5 *The gig is perfect for you*
It's a crap gig and no one else will do it.

6 *You'll love the gig and they are our favourite clients*
Means that you are guaranteed to hate the gig and if there are any problems the agents won't help you.

7 *You do a few old standards, don't you?*
The gig is in a retirement home and the sum of all the band members ages will still be less than the age of the youngest person there.

8 *The venue hasn't paid me yet*
Your cheque is not in the post.

9 *Your cheque is in the mail*
It's not.

10 *It's very exclusive*
You'll have an audience of five – max.

How do I stop agents and venues from breaking my contract?

The easiest way is to make them not want to. If you are a popular band or artist with a growing number of followers an agent or promoter won't want to break your contract.

What do I do if I break the contract?

If you are able to give the agent, promoter or venue plenty of notice ask them if they will agree to you terminating the contract. The more notice you can give the more likely you are to succeed, especially if you are able to present them with a solution instead of a problem. You could offer to find a suitable replacement band/artist for the gig in question or offer to reschedule your gig for another night. If they agree to the cancellation send them a revised agreement for them to sign notifying their acceptance. If the agent, promoter or venue do not agree to the cancellation and you fail to perform the engagement you will be in breach of contract and subject to any penalty that results. Commonly, in such a situation a venue or promoter is entitled to seek a claim from you to cover their loss of earnings. A venue frequently quantifies this figure by comparing their revenue figures with that of the same date of the previous year and will expect you to compensate them for the shortfall.

✳ TIP ✳

Labour Union members who fail to fulfill their contractual obligations may find themselves subject to disciplinary action from their union for bringing the union into disrepute. This can mean anything from a fine to suspension or expulsion for repeat offenders.

Should their be contracts between band members?

In recent times contracts between band members, and in particular, between each band member and their manager or management company, have become increasingly common. With so much financial investment required to successfully launch and maintain the careers of new bands and artists it is not hard to see why. There is too much at stake to risk having members leave prematurely. With image nowadays playing as great an importance as talent, these contracts often go into great detail regarding acceptable and unacceptable codes of public behaviour which all band members are expected to adhere to.

Do we need contracts between band members if we don't have management?

It could certainly be helpful in preventing problems in the long term. By drawing up a contract you will be able to make each band member clear, right from the outset, what their rights and responsibilities are. The following is a list of issues that might crop up:

Who owns the equipment?

Usually, when bands form, each musician joins bringing in his or her own equipment. As time progresses bands start to need more gear and end up buying equipment collectively, often using gig earnings to do so. At this stage there is now equipment jointly owned as well as individually owned. None of this becomes a problem until someone wishes to leave the band or there is a discrepancy over who owns what. It is helpful if everyone keeps track of purchases and also comes to some sort of agreement, in advance, regarding what should happen if a band member wishes to leave. The easiest solution would be for the remaining band members to buy out the leaving musician's share. If the equipment is not bought by the whole band whoever buys it should be recognised as being the owner.

Who will be responsible for the band's expenses?

Band expenses can be anything from union dues to equipment hire. If these are not shared equally the person who picks up the tab for them will probably ask for a greater share of the bands' earnings. Each member's share of expenses and earnings needs to be clarified from the start.

Who owns the rights to the band's self-penned songs?

Everyone who collaborates on a song is entitled to equal share of the copyright. Publishing is usually broken down into percentage splits. It could be 50% music, 50% lyrics or any other combination the songwriters agree upon. It might be that three of the band wrote the song and they decide one should get 40% for the lyrics, another 40% for the music and the third 20% for the middle eight. Some bands decide to split all royalties equally regardless of who wrote the songs. The Levellers guitarist, Simon believes that each musician is as valuable as the song writers and says of their decision to share royalties equally:

‘ I can't play drums, bass or fiddle, so we need each other to survive. ’ *Simon, Levellers Guitarist. (Band Magazine)*

Who owns the band's name if you have a change in line-up?

Deciding this in advance can spare everyone from potential lengthy and costly disputes later on. Your band contract should also state how much notice each member is required to give before leaving. It would be reasonable to ask for a minimum of two weeks notice, and is common for contracts to ask for more.

What if I own all the gear, the van and all the music we play is mine? Do I need a band contract?
No, but you need to make clear to each band member that they will not be able to claim any artistic interest in your material and that they are being 'hired' just to play the notes. To do this you will need to have them sign a 'talent release,' which confirms they agree to perform on this basis. This agreement will have to be made *before* you start working together.

Will I always be offered a contract?

Not always. This is what Steve Howard (Horns player with Ray Charles and Albert Collins) has to say on the subject:

' A lot of it is handshake agreement – has been in the past. When I worked with Albert Collins I didn't have a handshake agreement with him, I'd exchange a letter or something like that but then with Paul McCartney and bigger artists there is a contract, generally speaking. Because, the more the money is the more everybody wants to be secure. ' *Steve Howard (horns: Paul McCartney & Wings ('75-80), Ray Charles, Albert Collins).*

Advice clinic with Billy Hulting

Q What advice would you give musicians regarding contracts?

A I never signed a contract for a tour – Barry had the closest thing which was a letter of intent. I scratched off a lot of stuff, signed only what I wanted to, and turned it back in. Not much was said. Mostly you have what is referred to as a deal. You agree on a pay schedule and per diem and that's really all. Some of the super huge tours may have a retainer or contracts. One good thing to agree on is some sort of separation clause. Two weeks notice for cancellations. If they come under that two week thing then you should get paid. You also need to give them two weeks notice before you want to leave. They may hate the thought of this but it really benefits you both. If they argue against it (I had one management company try) just tell them that by their own definition you could show up at the airport and tell them you aren't going – that ought to switch them to your side.
Billy Hulting (percussion: Lou Rawls, Natalie Cole, Barry Manilow, Maynard Ferguson).

Musician's Unions: What do they offer?

The American Federation of Musicians (AFM) which represents North America and Canada, and Britain's Musician's Union (MU) are just two bodies which offer their musician members a tremendous network of support in all areas of the music industry.

Legal advice
Free and discounted legal assistance is available to all members with queries regarding musical employment.

Contract advice
Union members benefit from free vetting of contracts. Members can receive guidance on everything from contracts for live performances and recording, to managing and publishing contracts.

Rates
One of the union's obligations is to negotiate fees with broadcasting and non-broadcasting media on behalf of its members. This covers everything from TV, motion pictures, radio, video, record and compact disc, to interactive media.

Insurance
The Unions offer packages which cover their members for medical, equipment, and public liability insurance.

Recovery of unpaid fees
It is likely that every musician, at least once in their lifetime, will have a problem getting an agent or venue to pay up after they have completed a gig. The unions' legal departments help musicians recover unpaid fees.

How to contact them

Musician's Union

National Office
60-62 Clapham Road, London SW9 0JJ
Tel: 0171-582 5566
Fax: 0171-582 9805
Website: www.musiciansunion.org.uk

Scotland
11 Sandyford Place, Glasgow G3 7NB
Tel: 0141-248 3723
Fax: 0141-204 3510

North West
40 Canal Street, Manchester M1 3WD
Tel: 0161-236 1764
Fax: 0161-236 0159

Midlands
Benson House, Lombard Street, Digbeth,
Birmingham
B12 0QR
Tel: 0121-622 3870
Fax: 0121-622 5361

East
60-62 Clapham Road, London SW9 0JJ
Tel: 0171-582 5566
Fax: 0171-582 9805

North/North East
327 Roundhay Road, Leeds LS8 4HT
Tel: 0113-248 1335
Fax: 0113-248 1292

South East
60-62 Clapham Road, London SW9 0JJ
Tel: 0171-582 5566
Fax: 0171-582 9805

South West
131 St Georges Road, Bristol BS1 5UW
Tel: 0117-926 5438
Fax: 0117-925 3729

American Federation of Musicians

New York Headquarters
1501 Broadway
Suite 600
New York, NY
10036-5503
Tel: (212) 869-1330
Fax: 764-6134
e-mail:info@afm.org

West Coast Office
1777 North Vine St.
Suite 500
Hollywood, CA
90028-5268
Tel: (213) 461-3441
Fax: 462-8340
e-mail:info@afm.org

Canadian Office
75 The Donway West
Suite 1010
Don Mills, Ont.
M3C 2E9
Tel: (416) 391-5161
Fax: 391-5165
e-mail:canoff@afm.org

3
Travelling

* Protecting your gear
* Baggage limits
* Insurance
* Damaged equipment
* Hot and cold climates

*A*ny musician who has ever stayed behind after a gig and watched the roadies haul their gear off stage knows that second to their crew and the technicians – road cases are a musician's best friend. Even the most careful handling won't be enough to protect equipment from the sort of general wear and tear that touring presents.

'Gear just gets worn out and beat up on tour – it can't be avoided but the process can be slowed. Any compromise in selecting cases will have a direct effect on the safety of your gear.'
Billy Hulting (percussion: Lou Rawls, Natalie Cole, Barry Manilow, Maynard Ferguson).

How do I protect my gear?

Flight cases are the best way to protect your equipment. They are not cheap but they are far cheaper than replacing wrecked equipment, and could spare you the time-consuming inconvenience of being forced to hire and familiarise yourself with foreign gear at short notice should any equipment become damaged in transit.

The type of flight case you choose will depend on the type of touring you are doing. Today's flight cases come in semi-flight or full-flight design (sometimes described as light-flight or full-flight) which cover most touring needs. The good news is that the materials used now are lighter in comparison to their heavyweight counterparts of a few years ago but offer the same, if not greater, protection to your equipment. Flight cases go a long way to help protect your equipment but they by no means make your gear bullet proof. Equipment inside a flight case still doesn't fair very well when dropped from a fully extended fork lift truck, for example.

Where can I get flight cases made?

Pick up any music industry magazine and you'll usually find flight cases advertised in the magazine's classified ads section.

Advice clinic with Kevin Dukes

 Q How do you protect your gear when you are on the road?

 A I have all my gear fitted for flight quality cases, and pray for a good crew.' Kevin Dukes (guitar: Peter Cetera, Billy Joel).

I'm a solo musician and usually travel by air. How can I protect my gear and still keep under my baggage weight limit?

This can be quite a challenge even if you are not transporting a PA or amplifiers (which, as a solo musician you should aim to have the venue provide). If you are travelling within, or to, the USA you have the luxury of having a 70lb baggage limit to play with. This makes it quite an easy proposition. Even if you are carrying a keyboard in a semi-flight case this will probably only take up half of your allocation (around 18 kg or 40 lb). In Europe where you only have a 20 kg (44 lb) baggage allowance it's much harder.

If you are travelling over your weight allowance there are a couple of things you can do or try.

1 Ask your agent/promoter or the venue to arrange for an increased baggage allowance. Agents who regularly use airlines to transport their clients, or have local contacts, don't usually find this to be a problem, but they will need advance notice so don't leave your request to the last minute.
2 Ship anything you can do without ahead of you. But first check how long it will take to catch up with you. Surface mail might only take a few days but sea freighting could take anything from four to six weeks. Air freighting a small amount is often as expensive as paying excess baggage duty.

If you can't get your limit raised:

1 When you pack put any of the small but heavy items (power adapters, effects pedals etc.) into your carry-on luggage. Not the ideal situation but at times it might be your only option. If you are challenged by airline personnel on the weight of your carry-on piece, charm is your best tactic. Explaining that you are carrying tools of your trade can help but even if it doesn't, at worst they'll probably only insist your hand luggage goes into the hold and won't charge you excess duty.
2 If you are over your weight allowance at the check-in and the desk attendant wants to charge you be as nice as you can without being irritating. It might not make the attendant overlook the extra kilos but could at least encourage them to underestimate how many of them there are.

Is it safe for instruments to be placed in the hold?
It depends how much protection they have. Not only do they have to be protected against hard knocks but they also need to be protected against climate. The extreme low temperatures which occur in the hold are not good for natural materials like solid wood guitars.

Airlines usually let guitarists bring their instruments into the passenger cabin (which is climate and pressure controlled) as long as there is space and they are not in bulky cases. Keyboardists don't usually get granted the same facility though.

' I always carried my bass in a gig bag on board the plane where they put it in the coat closet, or it usually fits in the overhead bin. '
Carol Kaye (bass: Hampton Hawes).

Will my gear survive a trip on the luggage carousel?

In a well packed flight case, for a lot of gear it shouldn't be a problem. When you check in you can request it to be carried by hand or taken by trolley/cart to the aircraft instead of it going on the conveyor belt. You usually don't get the same service at your destination though, and the next time you get to see your beloved instrument is when it pops up onto the carousel. Make sure that your cases are not only solid but are also well padded inside, and cover the outside with *Fragile* stickers. Some equipment doesn't travel well though, no matter how well protected it is. Horns in particular should be taken as carry-on luggage wherever possible.

'I can guarantee you, if you check a horn on, even in a hard case – horns are such delicate instruments – especially saxophones. Check one on and it's gonna get messed up some kind of way because the airline people they just look at it as a piece of luggage, and they're just tossing it about, and it's really pretty dicey to be putting your horns in the luggage. Now some guys have anvil cases built that their horn case will actually fit into, you know, those padded steel cases. I have a trumpet case. It's made by a company called Reunion Blues. It's an instrument bag company, they make bags for guitars and saxophones and trumpets and everything – it's from San Francisco. A lot of the guys use these now and it's made ... my bag will hold a trumpet and a flugelhorn, plus I've got room for my mutes in there. It's a padded bag and it meets the requirements for size for a carry-on bag for the airlines so I can just take it anywhere I need to go with me.'
Steve Howard (horns: Paul McCartney, Ray Charles).

'I buy good-quality, custom-made cases, with reinforced corners. I make sure I go over with my tech exactly how my gear will be packed, where accessories will be stored, and we stuff any dead space with foam or toweling. I make sure every piece has my name stencilled on it.'
Julie Homi (keyboards: Robert Palmer, Yanni, Peter Cetera).

Insurance

Do I need to insure my equipment?

Unless you can easily afford to replace anything that gets lost, damaged or stolen and are prepared to take the gamble, the

TIP
Don't put heavy carry-on luggage in the overhead luggage bins on the plane. The bucket shape of the locker makes it almost impossible to retrieve and should the locker's catch spring open mid-flight (as they frequently do) your carry-on might fall out on you or a fellow passenger. Stow heavy bags underneath the seat in front of you.

TIP
When travelling make sure that any easily carried vital performing gear (such as music, ROM/RAM cards for sound modules etc.) are in your carry-on luggage. Then if your luggage gets waylaid you'll still be able to perform.

answer will be, yes. The next step will be to try and find an insurer who offers a policy which doesn't read like a Monty Python script. Read the fine print on some musical instrument insurance plans and it looks like the only time you will be covered is on the third day of the abalone fishing season, as long as it's during a full moon and falls on a day with an R in it. It is very difficult to get comprehensive equipment insurance.

Musical equipment insurance usually does *not* cover:

1 Anything from the first £25 ($40) to £250 ($400) of your claim, depending on your agreement.
2 Loss or damage caused by wear and tear.
3 Damage caused by negligent handling or faulty use. (i.e. dropping your equipment down a flight of stairs or blowing out the transformer by plugging into the wrong voltage).
4 Theft, loss or damage of any equipment left in a vehicle which isn't fully enclosed (such as a van); or theft, loss or damage of any instrument left in an enclosed vehicle which is left unlocked or unsecured. You will also not be covered if your equipment is in a secured vehicle which is left unattended for more than 30 minutes during the hours of darkness (between sunrise and sunset.) In the past some insurers also required you to immobilise the vehicle by removing the rotor arm or similar means – just what every musician feels like doing after a long gig.
5 Destruction or damage caused by extremes of temperature or climate.
6 Theft, loss or damage while your equipment is in anyone's possession other than your own.
7 Damage to your equipment caused by power surges or power leakages.
8 Damage caused by mechanical breakdown.
9 Loss or damage your equipment incurs while being repaired.

Loosely translated this tends to imply that the only time your equipment is insured is when it is stolen, in broad daylight, from a vehicle which you have made impossible to break into; or when the van has been blown up or gutted by fire – (as long as it isn't your fault).

'I carry my own musical instrument insurance, in addition to any insurance the tour may carry.'
Julie Homi (keyboards: Peter Cetera, Yanni, Robert Palmer).

How do I choose a good insurance company?
Your best bet is to shop around bearing in mind the above considerations. Most musicians' unions offer equipment insurance packages to their members, but again check the terms and conditions. For musicians who work from home most of the time you should be able to get some degree of cover by including your equipment on the household contents insurance policy.

Will my travel insurance cover my gear?
Most travel insurance policies exclude musical instruments or anything related so, no.

I'm thinking of shipping some of my gear ahead; will it be covered by freight forwarding or marine insurance?
Similar to travel insurance music related equipment is usually excluded and requires specialist insurance.

What do I do if I need to claim?
Hope your broker and/or your policy is as good as you thought it was. First you'll need to notify the broker or company of what has happened. If any goods have been stolen you will have to file a report at your local police station and provide your insurers or broker with a copy of the report. For damaged goods they will also require a detailed report explaining how the damage occurred and an assessment to determine whether the equipment is repairable.

So once I've done all that the insurance company will give me a cheque and that will be it, right?
Nice idea but it rarely happens that way. Insurance companies can be extremely tedious when it comes to settling claims. It frequently takes time and perseverance to achieve a satisfactory result, not to mention the ability to battle against what frequently appears to be baffling logic.

Having once freight forwarded my computer gear to later discover that the monitor hadn't travelled well (it rattled a lot when it arrived), I notified my insurance company only to discover that although I had transit cover with them they were not going to pay because they had determined the damage was the airline's responsibility. When I contacted the airline I found out that airlines don't think of cargo in terms of anything other than weight. As far as they were concerned 8 kilos of monitor had been dispatched and 8 kilos had been delivered so they had fulfilled their side of the agreement (even though the monitor would never fulfill its purpose again). Furthermore, they said that if I had wanted it to be in working order when it arrived it should have been packed better. Clearly they were disappointed that a flight case couldn't cope with a nose dive off the end of a fork lift. The good news is that after persevering to the point of being annoying they finally paid up.

What should I do if any of my equipment breaks down or gets damaged on tour?

First you have to assess the extent of the damage or breakdown. Often tours have technicians on their crew who, at moments like these, are worth ten times their salary. A good tech can pull off some remarkable repairs at short notice. It's amazing what they can do with a soldering iron and a roll of gaffer tape (duct tape).

If you don't have tech support and the repairs are beyond your capabilities you will have to either recruit local help or beg, borrow or hire replacement gear. If your agent/promoter is contactable they might have a local contact who will be able to help you find what you need. If not, your next best bet is asking the venue's booking agent or the resident engineer.

What gear should I take with me?

Your pre-tour rehearsals and the size of the venues you will be playing will help you decide this one. It is always tempting to take every piece of gear you own just in case you need it, but the restrictions of space, time and the cost of hauling stuff around usually mean that each band member has to take the barest set-up they can get away with. Those with the toughest decisions to make are most often keyboard players, drummers and percussionists, who tend to believe it's not possible ever to have too much gear on the road with them.

❛ Figure out what you actually need. Take into account which songs need what effects, which instruments, etc. Consider the type of support the tour has. If the tech support is going to be stressed (i.e. spread too thin, each crew member doing too many things), it would be better to take a set-up that is really easy to setup and maintain. Try not to take valuable, 'vintage' or otherwise hard-to-replace items unless you absolutely have to. Of course, this is a tough call sometimes, and everybody has to make their own choices. You may have cut that fabulous 8-bar solo in the studio on a rare '59 green Strat, but live most people just aren't going to know the difference. I try to take instruments that are really good, but are not irreplacable.*

Benny Rietveld (bass: Santana, Sheila E, Miles Davis).

Now I don't take any more than I need to do the gig the best I can. This will differ from gig to gig. If you have techs out who will be setting up your gear you can make them very unhappy by bringing a lot of stuff out with you that you really just don't need. Sure – you want your setup to look cool (especially true for drummers and percussionists) but you really don't want to hang the guys up too much.

I'm sure if the techs for Natalie Cole read this they'll be laughing – I used this huge cage with everything hanging on it – eight cymbals, drumKAT and malletKAT with loads of external triggers and stuff. I used it all and believe it was very effective – Natalie's gig covered a lot of musical territory. She also did a good number of ballads and I felt the artistic need to make the percussion parts a little different on each, so I think the large set-up was justified. Big racks for percussionists were just coming into style then – I used to tell Natalie that every star as big as she deserved to have a percussionist with a really cool setup!*

Billy Hulting (percussion: Lou Rawls, Natalie Cole, Maynard Ferguson).

If you are not in the habit of carrying your own spares kit for your gear this is probably a good time to start. There are three vital elements which no survival kit should be without – a set of tools (screw-drivers, allen keys, pliers – whichever is suitable for your equpment), the kind of selection of batteries that Woolworth's would be proud of, and the biggest life and credibility saver of them all – gaffer (duct) tape. A famous session drummer who wishes to remain nameless says:

I once turned up at a gig and discovered I'd left my bass pedal behind. I didn't have time to go back and get it so I gaffer taped a screw-driver to my foot and played the gig like that instead. Anonymous.

In its time gaffer tape has been used for everything from making emergency repairs to broken guitar straps and torn clothing; patching broken instrument cases; and holding down adventurous sustain pedals which forever keep sliding out of a keyboard player's reach requiring them to play at an inclined 45 degree angle – to name just a few. Sometimes gaffer tape even gets used for the more mundane purposes for which it was first thought to be designed, such as taping down cables.

Creative uses of gaffer tape

1 I had myself gaffer taped. I was doing a guitar solo alone and there were like seven or eight spotlights on me, and the crew ran out, tucked my arms behind my back and duct taped my arms and laid me on the ground with those spotlights on me as someone else behind my amps played the guitar solo. I know of other uses of duct tape but I try not to go into them … It's pretty strange.
Bobby Messano (guitar: Steve Winwood, Robin Beck).

2 The most creative use of gaffer tape would be as a boob-support. I'm sure I'm not the only woman who has used it when I've forgotten my bra, or when I didn't want those unsightly bra straps to show.
Julie Homi (keyboards: Peter Cetera, Yanni, Robert Palmer).

3 Sealing a musician into his room by running gaffer tape round the frame of the door.
Martin Jenner (guitar: Cliff Richard, Everly Brothers).

Cold climates/hot climates

Travelling in areas which experience extreme climactic conditions need extra consideration.

Hot climates
Electrical equipment gets hot enough even in mild temperatures. If you are performing in hot locations – particularly if you are outdoors, you will need to make sure your equipment is prevented from overheating. Cooling fans, placed around the equipment, can be particularly effective.

Cold climates
Any musician who has gigged across Canada in the middle of winter knows that sub-zero conditions have a habit of interfering with your schedule. Not only can wintry weather cause travel delays but once you arrive at your destination you also have to allow time for your equipment – particularly the cables and leads, to thaw out. Cables become brittle when exposed to extreme cold and will snap if handled before they

TIP
If you are not used to working in hot environments make sure that besides your equipment you also prevent yourself from overheating. Drink lots of fluids (preferably not alcoholic), before and after the gig to avoid dehydrating. Heat stroke is extremely unpleasant and can be potentially life endangering if ignored, but is easily prevented by making sure you take sufficient fluids on board.

have had a chance to warm up. Instruments also require extra care in cold conditions.

' Instruments will get out of tune. And certain horns, like a saxophone – you wouldn't want it to stay out in the heat, or the extreme cold for very long; so too with woodwind instruments because the corks and pads and stuff will loosen up. It's something to be considered but generally speaking horn players – we keep our horns in our own possession at all times. We don't put them on an equipment truck or something like that and send them off with somebody. My horn is in the hotel room with me all the time, or the airport, it's only out in cold for limited time.

When we were with McCartney I played trumpet and flugelhorn, and we had one of the other horn section guys play two different saxophones and a flute on the concert. He had to make a quick switch between horns and one of the things that was happening was that when you'd pick up that other horn, after it had been sitting for a long time, especially in a lot of European concert halls that sometimes tend to be colder – especially in the winter months, they don't have as much heat in there, so the horn would probably be ten degrees colder and so it's extremely out of tune whenever you pick it up and start to play it immediately without having to blow some air through it and warm it up. So we had a big, giant heating blanket that sat on an equipment crate that was right behind the horn riser and we would put those horns in there – wrap them up in that little heating blanket to keep them warm, then whenever you got ready to play you just picked it up and it was warm and it stayed in tune.'
Steve Howard (horns: Paul McCartney & Wings, Ray Charles, Albert Collins).

Travelling *Checklist*

✔ Protect your gear
✔ Have adequate insurance cover
✔ Be prepared for hot and cold climates
✔ Carry anything vital to your performance (ROM and RAM cards etc.,) in your hand luggage.
✔ If you have minimal tech support, take an emergency tool kit. Don't forget the Gaffer tape!

4
Your health on the road

* Medical/health issues   * Medical insurance
* Nasty diseases   * The rock & roll lifestyle

Medical/health issues and AIDS free certificates

Planning ahead

If you are about to be touring abroad check whether the
countries you are visiting have any health requirements. A
surprising number do. There are even parts of Europe where
visitors are recommended to be immunised against Hepatitis A,
Polio and Typhoid. If you are touring the Middle East, Africa or
Asia the list extends to include Malaria, Yellow fever, Meningitis,
and recently, Diphtheria. The good news is that most of the
inoculations are long lasting. Once you are Immunised against
Yellow Fever and Polio, for example, you are covered for ten
years. Protection against Hepatitis though only lasts for six
months.

Nasty diseases and how you can get them

Hepatitis A

Caught by: most often caught by drinking or eating contaminated water or food.

Symptoms: fever, headache, chills, tiredness. Later this may progress to a general lack of appetite, abdominal pain and sickness. Other symptoms include dark coloured urine and a yellowing of the skin (jaundice).

Treatment: rest, drinking plenty of fluids and eating, in moderation, non-fatty foods.

How prevented: immunisation with a gamma globulin injection and by taking the extra precaution of eating only in sanitary conditions.

Polio

Caught by: drinking or eating contaminated water or food.

Symptoms: flu-like symptoms and aching limbs.

How prevented: Most people receive immunisation during early childhood. Adults may require a booster which is administered painlessly (usually the vaccine is placed on a sugar lump for you to swallow).

Typhoid

Caught by: drinking or eating contaminated water or food.

Symptoms: in the early stages the symptoms are flu-like causing a headache, fever, and sore throat.

Treatment: antibiotics. Medical help must be sought because Typhoid can lead to other complications such as pneumonia and peritonitis.

How prevented: immunisation by injection.

Malaria

Caught by: being bitten by an infected mosquito. Malaria victims suffer from recurring fevers, and other complications which can be fatal.

Symptoms: recurring headaches, fevers and profuse sweating.

How prevented: avoid insect bites by wearing insect repellent and by taking anti-malarial medication. This needs to be taken for two weeks before you leave and for four weeks after your return.

Yellow fever

Caught by: being bitten by an infected mosquito.

How prevented: immunisation by vaccination.

Meningitis

Contracted by: close contact with an infected person who can pass it on through coughs and sneezes. Immediate treatment is required as the condition can be fatal.

Symptoms: severe headache, fever, skin rash, sensitivity to light, and stiffness in the neck.

Treatment: large doses of antibiotic.

How prevented: immunisation of certain strains is possible with a vaccination

Diphtheria

Caught by: close contact with an infected person who can spread the disease through coughs and sneezes.

Symptoms: skin infection; throat infection

How prevented: immunisation with a low dose vaccine.

HIV/AIDS (human immuno-deficiency virus – acquired immune deficiency syndrome)

Can be passed on by:

∗ Having unprotected sex with an infected person.
∗ Using infected syringes
∗ Being treated with infected dental equipment or any contaminated instrument which punctures the skin (such as tattooing or acupuncture needles).
∗ A transfusion with infected blood.

How prevented: There is no vaccination or cure.

∗ Avoid casual sex.
∗ If you do have sex with a new partner use a condom.
∗ Don't inject non-prescribed drugs.
∗ Don't have a tattoo or your ears pierced if you can't be sure the equipment is sterile.

TIP

Take a supply of condoms with you as these may not be readily available or of a good enough quality elsewhere.

'Condoms – when you first get on the road you will be overwhelmed with this new power you have. Everyone notices it but few like to talk about it or admit it. Be prepared – you will immediately be more attractive to potential sexual partners then you were before.'
Billy Hulting (percussion: Lou Rawls, Natalie Cole, Barry Manilow, Maynard Ferguson).

To find out what immunisation you require (if any) check with either your doctor, or travel agent, or contact the Embassy or High Commission of the countries you are entering. Here's a general guideline of current requirements. These are subject to frequent changes though so check the requirements at the time of travel.

Immunisation checklist

Country	Hepatitis A Polio Typhoid	Malaria	Yellow Fever	Meningitis/ Diphtheria
Argentina	*	*		
Australia			E	
Bahamas	*		E	
Bahrain	*			
Belarus	*			
Bosnia/Hercegovina	*			
Brazil	*	*	E*	
Brunei	*		E	
Bulgaria	*			
Canada				
Chile	*			
China	*	*	E*	
Costa Rica	*	*		
Croatia	*			
Czech & Slovak Rep.	*			
Egypt	*		E	
Gabon	*	*	E+	
Greece			E	
Hong Kong	*			
Hungary				
India	*	*	E	M
Indonesia	*	*	E	
Japan	*			
Korea	*			
Kuwait	*			
Latvia				
Lebanon	*		E	
Malaysia	*	*	E	

Immunisation checklist (cont)

Country	Hepatitis A Polio Typhoid	Malaria	Yellow Fever	Meningitis/ Diphtheria
Mexico	*	*	E	
Morocco	*			
New Zealand				
Philippines	*	*	E	
Poland				
Qatar	*		E	
Romania	*			
Russia				D
Saudi Arabia	*	*	E	M
Singapore	*		E	
Slovenia	*			
South Africa	*	*	E	
Sri Lanka	*	*	E	
Switzerland				
Taiwan	*		E	
Thailand	*	*	E	
Tunisia	*		E	
Turkey	*	*		
United Arab Emirates	*	*		
Ukraine				D
Uruguay	*			
USA				
Venezuela	*	*	*	
Vietnam	*	*	E	
Yugoslavia	*			

(Information correct at time of going to press but subject to change)

Key

* =   Immunisation recommended.

E =   Immunisation mandatory if you have passed through an area where Yellow Fever is present.

E+ = Immunisation essential.

D =   Check you've been immunised against Diphtheria.

M =   Meningitis

Medicines

Certain medications are not always easily available abroad so If you require prescribed medicines and are about to start a lengthy tour aim to take a supply which will last until your return home. At the same time though, check that there are no restrictions on bringing the medication into the countries you are visiting. Some medicines available over the counter in your home country may be controlled substances elsewhere. If you think you are going to have a problem take a letter from your doctor which explains why you need the particular drug or drugs you will be carrying. It doesn't take any imagination at all to guess what can happen to you if a customs officer finds a musician in front of them who happens to be carrying their own virtual pharmacy.

> ✳ ✳ ✳
> ✳ **TIP** ✳
> If you do need immunisation give your doctor as much notice as possible as some inoculations cannot be given at the same time as others. Some also take time to become effective.

Dental check-ups

It sounds tedious but if you are going to be away for a long time or haven't had a check-up recently, do so before the tour. If you develop a problem on the road and have a tight schedule it could be some time before you can arrange treatment. It will also be cheaper having it done at home.

First aid kits

Many travel representatives recommend travellers to take emergency medical travel kits with them. Typically these will contain surgical tape, non-stick dressings, sterilised swabs, syringes and needles. This type of medical kit is probably highly suitable for every traveller *except* musicians. To say that customs and immigration officials don't like them is an understatement. To be a musician and carrying this kind of kit is much like saying 'Please deport me.' They will be only too happy to oblige but will probably wish to body search (cavity search) you before doing so.

❛ I had taken syringes and needles into Korea because I knew I was going to have to have an AIDS test while I was there as part of the visa requirement. Not being sure how safe local supplies were my doctor had recommended I take some with me. It never occurred to me that carrying them would cause a problem. It didn't in Korea but it did months later when I was entering the US. When the Customs officer searching my case found a pack of needles and syringes that was it! – I was hauled off to a side room and interrogated for five hours. I thought , 'now I'm for it – here comes the body search. Any minute now a terrifying looking government official wearing surgical gloves is going to come in and ask me to bend over.' Lucky for me it never quite came to that. I think it helps if you look about as intimidating as Doris Day but it was not a fun experience. I was also detained so long I missed all my connections and had to spend a night in the airport lounge so I won't do that again. ❞ *Stella Hemmings.*

AIDS free certificates

It's becoming increasingly commonplace for musicians (and all professional travellers) to have to provide a certificate which proves you are HIV or AIDS free before being granted a work permit – particularly in the Middle East and Asia. Although this tends to be a requirement more for long term would-be residents (those working for a month or more), than for short term visitors it still presents a dilemma. If you don't provide the certificate you won't get the work permit.

To get the certificate you either have to have a blood test at home or be tested on arrival in the country. Most people would prefer to be tested at home but there are a couple of other factors to consider. Some doctors will not give you an AIDS blood test without you first attending counselling sessions. Their concern is to make sure you are prepared as much as is possible in case the test result comes back positive. Even if you are quite sure you have not been in contact with the virus they will still not conduct the blood test without this proviso. Also, once it appears on your medical records that you have had an AIDS blood test you might experience difficulties getting life insurance. Insurance companies are not interested about any other reasons for why you have had the test. To them having the test indicates that you believe you have been exposed to the virus and in their eyes that implies you have an undesirable lifestyle and makes you a riskier liability. If at the time you need to provide an AIDS free certificate these problems still exist you might prefer to have the test done abroad where the records stay in that country or are destroyed when you leave (assuming you are not intending to make that country your permanent residence).

Medical insurance

Depending where you are in the world the cost of emergency medical care can be anything from exorbitant to virtually free. Citizens of any of the EEA countries (European Economic Area) can take advantage of the reciprocal medical service arrangements between each member states, as well as Iceland, Liechtenstein and Norway. Before you leave visit your local Department of Health and Social Security (DHSS) office, or your equivalent department, and pick up form E111 for each crew/band member. These need to be filled out and then taken to a Post Office to receive validation stamps. The E111 is issued free of charge. Take it with you when you travel within the EEA.

What the E111 entitles you to
If you are taken ill or have an accident while visiting an EEA country the Form E111 will enable you to receive free or reduced cost emergency treatment. This is state provided and will mean that you receive treatment on the same terms as the citizens of the country you are visiting. Private treatment is not covered.

Charges for treatment
Each EEA country sets its own rules when it comes to charges for state medical care. Some treatment is free. In some cases you will need to pay for part of the costs, and in others you may have to pay for all of the costs and then apply for a refund of either some or all of the charges.

How the reciprocal health care scheme works in each country

Austria
Where to go for information: Your local Regional Health Insurance Office
Documents you'll need: Passport
How to find a doctor or a dentist: Contact the Regional Health Insurance Office
Hospital treatment: In a public hospital where you will receive standard class treatment.
Cost: Low. Most treatment will be covered by vouchers issued by the health insurance scheme. For hospital stays a small daily charge will be made.

> **∗ TIP ∗**
> If you are travelling within France, Germany, Italy, The Netherlands or Spain, it is worthwhile taking a photocopy of your E111 Form as those countries will require the photocopy if you need to apply for treatment.

Belgium
Where to go for information: The regional offices of the Auxiliary Fund For Sickness and Invalidity Insurance or the office of Local Sickness Funds.

Documents you'll need: Passport, Form E111

How to find a doctor or a dentist: Consult any doctor or dentist and show your Form E111. You will be charged for treatment so obtain a receipt.

Hospital treatment: Take Form E111 to a local Sickness Office for them to authorise payment of some of the hospital costs.

Cost: A refund of approximately 75% is given for approved treatment. Apply to a sickness office with your receipts, copies of prescriptions and Form E111.

Denmark
Where to go for information: The Social and Health Department of the local council

Documents you'll need: Passport

How to find a doctor or a dentist: Consult any. Show your passport and if charged obtain a receipt.

Hospital treatment: Free

Cost: Free. For refunds apply to your local council with your receipts before you leave Denmark.

Finland
Where to go for information: Local Offices of the Sickness Insurance Department

Documents you'll need: Passport or E111

How to find a doctor or dentist: Contact a local Municipal Health Centre.

Hospital treatment: In a public hospital.

Cost: Standard fees which are not refundable are charged for most consultations and treatment. For hospital care there is a fixed daily charge which is also non-refundable.

France
Where to go for information: The local Sickness Insurance Office

Documents you'll need: Passport, E111

How to find a doctor or a dentist: Ask to be put in contact with a doctor or dentist who works within the French Insurance system.

Hospital treatment: In a public hospital.

Cost: A refund of approximately 75% is given for approved treatment. You pay first and then apply to the local sickness office for the refund which will be sent to your home address later.

Germany

Where to go for information: Any medical insurance company. You need them to give you a credit/transfer settlement form before you can receive treatment (without it you will be charged).

Documents you'll need: Form E111.

How to find a doctor or a dentist: Ask the insurance company for their list of approved doctors and dentists.

Hospital treatment: In the event of an emergency admission give your Form E111 to the hospital's administration department and ask them to apply for the appropriate forms on your behalf.

Cost: With the correct paperwork treatment is free except for a small daily charge for stays in hospital.

Gibraltar

Where to go for information: Gibraltar Health Authority.

Documents you'll need: Passport, E111.

How to find a doctor or a dentist: Contact Casemates Health Centre.

Hospital treatment: St. Bernard's Hospital.

Cost: Virtually free. You will have to pay in full for dental treatment.

Greece

Where to go for information: The Social Insurance Institute (IKA)

Documents you'll need: Passport, E111

How to find a doctor or a dentist: Contact your local IKA clinic.

Hospital treatment: In a IKA hospital.

Cost: Varies. If there is no local IKA facility you may have to pay the full cost of private treatment and then apply to a central IKA office for a refund.

Iceland

Where to go for information: State Social Security Institute. Tel: 5604400

Documents you'll need: Form E111.

How to find a doctor or a dentist: Contact the local health centre.

Hospital treatment: In-patient treatment is free as long as you present a Form E111.

Cost: Standard non-refundable fee for out patient treatment. You will have to pay in full for dental treatment.

Ireland (Republic)

Where to go for information: Your local Health Board.

Documents you'll need: Evidence of your permanent address e.g. driving license.

How to find a doctor or a dentist: Contact the local Health Board and ask to be put in contact with a doctor or dentist who works within the public health service.

Hospital treatment: Has to be approved by the Health Board to avoid charges.

Cost: Normally free.

Italy

Where to go for information: The Local Health Unit (USL) and ask for a certificate of entitlement.

Documents you'll need: Passport, E111

How to find a doctor or a dentist: Ask the USL to provide you with a list of their practitioners.

Hospital treatment: In a public hospital you will receive standard class treatment.

Cost: Without the vouchers and certificates you will have to pay for everything and may find it difficult to get the refunds. You can receive reduced cost treatment in specified hospitals.

Liechtenstein

Where to go for information: National Office of Economy

Documents you'll need: Passport, E111.

How to find a doctor or a dentist: Contact any.

Hospital treatment: Only one hospital in Liechtenstein.

Cost: A standard fee may be charged. To claim refunds send your receipts and Form E111 to the National Office of Economy.

Luxembourg

Where to go for information: The Sickness Insurance Fund for Manual Workers

Documents you'll need: Passport

How to find a doctor or a dentist: Contact any.

Hospital treatment: Normally free but subject to a daily charge which is not refunded.

Cost: You must pay for all treatment and apply to the local Sickness Fund Office for a refund.

Netherlands
Where to go for information: Local Health Insurance Fund
Documents you'll need: Form E111.
How to find a doctor or a dentist: Ask to be put in contact with a
doctor who practices within the health insurance scheme.
Hospital treatment: Free hospital In-patient treatment when
authorised by the health insurance fund, (recognised locally as
ANOZ Verzekeringen).
Cost: Doctors services are usually free. You must pay dental
treatment in full.

Norway
Where to go for information: Local Sickness Offices.
Documents you'll need: Passport, E111.
How to find a doctor or a dentist: Ask to be put in contact with a
doctor who has a reimbursement agreement with the National
Insurance Administration (fortunately most doctors do).
Hospital treatment: Free.
Cost: You will be expected to pay a proportion of the costs of
your non-hospital treatment. You must pay dental treatment
in full.

Portugal
Where to go for information: Regional Health Service Offices
Documents you'll need: Passport, E111.
How to find a doctor or a dentist: Contact the Health Centre
Services and ask to be treated under the European
Community's arrangements.
Hospital treatment: You are required to pay for X-Rays and Lab
tests.
Cost: A non-refundable fixed fee for doctors' services. You must
pay dental treatment in full.

Spain
Where to go for information: District Offices of the National Social
Security Institute
Documents you'll need: Passport, E111.
How to find a doctor or a dentist: Contact your local health centre
or hospital clinic and ask for a doctor who practices within
the Spanish health care system.
Hospital treatment: Only free in a public hospital. Make sure they
are aware you wish to be treated under the EEA scheme or
you will be charged.
Cost: Approved doctors will provide treatment at low cost. You
must pay dental treatment costs in full.

Sweden
Where to go for information: Local Social Insurance Offices
Documents you'll need: Passport, E111.
How to find a doctor or a dentist: Contact a public insurance
affiliated practitioner. Hospital treatment: In-patient
treatment is free apart from a standard daily charge.
Cost: A standard non-refundable fee. You must pay dental
treatment costs in full.
For non-EEC citizens or anyone travelling outside the European
Community you will be advised to take out comprehensive
medical insurance. For non-USA citizens, North America is
one of the most expensive territories when it comes to
emergency (or otherwise) health care. Even the briefest of
visits to a hospital there will run up a bill of frightening
proportions.

Who should arrange medical insurance?

Most often it will be down to you. You can always ask your
agent or promoter to provide you with medical insurance cover
as part of your contract but generally they are unlikely to, and if
they do you should ask to see a copy of the policy before you
leave to make sure it is providing adequate cover.

Where can I get medical insurance?
Union members can obtain medical insurance through their
union. Contact your local branch secretary to find out more
details. For non-union members one of the easiest ways to obtain
insurance is either through your own insurance broker or your
local travel agent. In most instances you are able to buy
insurance from travel agents even if your travel arrangements
have not been made with them.

How is medical insurance calculated?
How much you pay for your insurance very much depends on
the countries you are visiting. Insurance is broken up into zones.
The cost of your cover is directly related to the cost of emergency
medical treatment in that zone.

If you are touring abroad a lot your best bet will be to take
out a business person's travel insurance policy. These policies are
designed for any one who travels abroad for frequent, but short
term periods on business trips. As an indication of the type of
package you can expect these policies often cover you for six
months travel in any one year as long as each trip is not longer

TIP
Warning: Form E111 covers basic medical care and may not cover all of your expenses (such as bringing someone home in the event of illness). You may wish to consider taking out additional insurance to cover these types of eventuality.

TIP
If you are touring abroad a lot your best bet will be to take out a business person's travel insurance policy. These policies are designed for any one who travels abroad for frequent, but short term periods on business trips. As an indication of the type of package you can expect these policies often cover you for six months travel in any one year as long as each trip is not longer than the period specified in the agreement (often around 60 days). This means that as long as you are making business trips and are not permanently living abroad you will have medical insurance cover for any emergency treatment you may need in the country you are visiting.

than the period specified in the agreement (often around 60 days). This means that as long as you are making business trips and are not permanently living abroad you will have medical insurance cover for any emergency treatment you may need in the country you are visiting.

The rock and roll lifestyle

Ever since the first troubadour took to the road a musician's lifestyle has been deemed to be one of sex and drugs and rock and roll. Unquestionably, musicians tend to move in circles where all three are available if they want them to be. Not only will there be people around who will be glad to get hold of anything you ask for, but on a well paid tour you will have the means and the money to make use of their resources. Whether you choose to or not is up to each individual to decide.

When drugs become a problem

It may be that a fellow band member or your agent or manager will think you have a problem long before it occurs to you. Whether you get due warning or not, if drug use starts to affect not only your ability to work, but also the quality of your performance you'll know that something needs to be done to safeguard your career as much as your long term health.

These days more and more resources are available for those who want to make use of them. In America the AFM (American Federation of Musicians) has set up the Musicians Assistance Program (MAP) for just this purpose. They provide funding and

Advice clinic with Tim Scott

Q What advice would you give to people regarding drugs and alcohol?

A It's really hard to say. Because I'm a member of a twelve step group I do a lot of speaking to people about that and especially to adolescents. And it's really hard to tell kids, you know, don't do this. At that age I know that I wouldn't listen to anybody about it. 'Cos I was just getting started, and I had to do about 25 years of research before I found out that it didn't work for me. I guess the only advice I could say is 'be careful.' Don't let it get out of hand.'

Q Is it easier for it to get out of hand when you are on tour?

A Towards the end of my using I acquired a nasty habit, and when you're out on the road it's very difficult to acquire and stay well. It was a problem for me on many occasions. So you just end up being sick – and it really detracts from the whole experience. You want to be conscious, do the job and enjoy yourself.

assistance specifically for musicians to help them get back on track. If you are not an AFM member check with your local musician's union branch to see if they are operating similar programs. If they are not, your GP will be aware of the programs running in your neighbourhood and will be able to provide you with a list of contacts to choose from.

Advice clinic with Tim Scott

What happened for me was my band did what's called an 'intervention' with me and they said that I was out of control and they were concerned about me, and they wanted me to get some help. They had this guy named Buddy Arnold – Buddy Arnold is the Head of the Musicians Assistance Program and he came and facilitated the intervention and got me into a treatment. What MAP does is they get funds from the record companies to support drug rehabilitation programs for musicians because most musicians – by the time they get to the point where they need help, they can't afford it – because there's no health insurance for us. We get nothing to fall back on, so this group probably saved my life, and I know that they have for a whole bunch of my friends.
And so it's very worth mentioning that if there's anybody out there in music and they're having a tough time and they don't know what to do, they should call them.

Q Were you resistant to getting that help at the time or were you ready for it?

A I was ready. I was really beat up and I was ready, I just didn't know what to do or where to turn.

Q How did the organisation help?

A They have a couple of facilities out in the desert that they refer people to and they provide as much funding as they can for it. In my case they did a co-pay with Riverside County, and sent me out to the desert. And it was the best thing that I ever did for myself. And afterwards they've got a private after care program where they have sober living facilities you can go to if you're not quite ready to come home, or go wherever you're gonna go, or if you've lost everything and you have nowhere to go, you can go there. And they have an encounter kind of therapy group twice a week. They work out of the musicians union. They have some licensed therapists that facilitate these groups, and they hold benefits around town with people like Bonnie Raitt and Natalie Cole performing and it's a really great organisation. I'm very grateful to them.
Tim J. Scott (bass: Stevie Wonder, Tower of Power).

Health on the road
Checklist

- ✔ Check inoculation requirements
- ✔ Visit your dentist
- ✔ Do you need an AIDS free certificate?
- ✔ Arrange medical insurance

5
Money

* Getting paid
* Where to keep it
* Choosing your currency

* Getting money home
* Running out of money
* Paying the bills

Ask any musician what they like best about touring and the chances are that getting paid will be pretty high on their list.

*"*Traveling ... getting paid ... seeing the country ... and the world ... getting paid ... meeting people ... making friends ... and fans ... getting paid. Playing every night can get your chops up. Did I mention gettin' paid?*"*
Gene Williams (keyboards: tours: Roberta Flack, Chaka Khan, Joe).

Getting paid

If you are a musician on a record company or management supported tour you will probably have your salary paid directly into your bank account at home, as part of your agreement. As long as money keeps going into your account you won't need to give it another thought, but if your gig abroad is a residency in a hotel or club which has been arranged through a booking agent you will usually be paid in cash either by the venue or your local entertainment agency representative.

Where to keep your money

For residencies which last more than a few weeks, either take out a safety deposit box in your hotel (a service which many hotels provide for free), or find out if you can rent a safety deposit box in a local bank. For long term engagements you may want to open a bank account. Most countries allow foreigners to open bank accounts without any trouble and all you need is to show them your passport to do so (occasionally they will ask you to state who your employer is over there). Banks, on the whole are always keen to welcome new customers wherever in the world you are. The only drawback to a bank account is that it will usually have to be in the local currency. Sometimes it is possible to open a foreign currency account though, so it is worthwhile asking.

Choosing your currency

Just as turbulence always strikes nanoseconds after the cabin crew serves drinks on a plane, you can guarantee that as soon as you know you are going to be travelling, the foreign exchange money markets will start behaving erratically. The easiest way to deal with this kind of turbulence is to arrange to be paid in your home currency. At least then your dollar (or whichever currency yours is) will still be worth a dollar at home. When that isn't possible you should aim to be paid in one of the major international currencies rather than the local currency of the country you are working in. Pick the one which will give you the best exchange rate when you get home. Often this will be US dollars, deutschmarks, or pounds sterling. There are several reasons for doing this:

1 Major currencies tend to be more stable than local ones when it comes to foreign exchange markets. This means that, in theory, sticking to a major currency should prevent you from losing out if the local currency should suddenly take a dip on the money markets.

TIP

Don't leave your passport, money or any other valuables in your luggage or hotel room. Even top class hotels can't guarantee the safety of your personal belongings left unattended in your room.

2 Some countries don't allow you to take their currency out of the country.

3 You will get such a bad exchange rate between the local currency and the currency at home that you wouldn't want to take it out of the country anyway.

Will I always be better off choosing a major currency?
Usually, but not necessarily always. Some domestic currencies are fixed or pegged to a major international currency and don't fluctuate anyway, so getting paid in those wouldn't be a problem.

Don't forget: the currency you wish to be paid in should be specified in your contract. Even when it is, you'll still find some agents will try to make their payments to you in the local currency instead because it's cheaper for them to do so. It's better that they pay for the conversion rather than you having to do it yourself later, unless, of course, the exchange rate between the local currency and your home currency suddenly changes and you can get a better deal by doing so (weirder things have happened).

Getting money home

In an era where instant communication across the world is possible at the click of a mouse, you would think that transferring money into your bank account at home, for a reasonable cost, would be a piece of cake. Sadly not so. The fee for making a bank to bank transfer can be horribly high, and the cost of converting it into travellers cheques can be almost as bad. You might be able to negotiate a more reasonable deal wiring money back but wiring services are not always easy to locate and not every country has them.

It sounds like dumb advice on the surface but unless you want to spend several hundred dollars on commission or transaction fees the cheapest way to get your money home is by taking it as cash. This is rarely as risky as it sounds as long as you keep the money close to hand (a money belt can work well), and don't draw attention to it. On the other hand though you may decide that spending a few hundred dollars in fees worth it for a worry free journey and to know that your money will already be in your account by the time you get home.

* TIP *
Choosing your currency can be a bit like trying to pick the winning number in a lottery, and you can pretty much guarantee that, the rules of the road being what they are, there will be times when even your stable currency of choice will fall down the exchange rate toilet. But don't panic – what goes down usually comes back up again if you can afford to wait!

* TIP *
Warning: Some governments are sensitive about large amounts of currency leaving the country. Check the restrictions of the country you are leaving and plan accordingly.

Running out of money

It happens. And the longer away from home you are going to be the more difficult it is to predict how much you will need to take with you. Your pay-cheque may get delayed during a holiday period; or you over-run on a couple of long distance phone calls to partners and friends and put a serious hole in your budget; or you might suddenly find yourself on the receiving end of an unexpectedly high bill like Bush's singer, Gavin Rossdale's girlfriend did on a visit to Jamaica.

> ' She called up this guy who was over and asked him to help with her hairstyle – he invoiced her for three grand. '
> *Gavin Rossdale on his girlfriend Gwen Stefani, singer with No Doubt (Sunday Times Magazine).*

Purchases are easily covered by your credit card but to get cash with it is expensive. At times like these American Express offers its members a service which would be great for others to copy. Walk into virtually any American Express office in the world with your passport and cheque book and you'll be able to write out a cheque, in your home currency, use your Amex card as a cheque guarantee card, and have it cashed in local currency. There is a restriction on how much you can cash (around £500/$750 in any one month) but it's great for emergencies (as long as you don't come across Gwen Stefani's hairdresser). You usually get a decent exchange rate too.

Paying the bills

Once you get caught up in the day to day demands of a tour it will be all too easy to forget about money matters at home. If you have bills that will need to be paid while you are gone, arrange for someone to do so for you until your return. Fewer things will put an end to your post tour euphoria quicker than finding you have a bunch of red bills, and threatening letters waiting for you as soon as you walk through the door.

Most musicians would find it hard to top one of singer-songwriter, Joan Armatrading's post tour experiences. It was reported that she once returned from tour and was immediately arrested for non-payment of taxes. Other similar stories abound. In Q Magazine Tom Doyle wrote that following The Verve's 1994-95 tour Richard Ashcroft returned home to Wigan to find that his landlord had changed the door locks on his rented flat and confiscated his possessions. He owed £3000 ($5000) in overdue rent at the time.

Your money

Checklist

✔ Choose your currency

✔ Make sure your contract clearly states how and when you will be paid

✔ Open a bank account or safety deposit box

✔ Arrange for someone to pay the bills at home

6
Psychology of surviving life on the road

- ✳ How to survive irritating band members
- ✳ Letting off steam
- ✳ Going solo
- ✳ What to expect
- ✳ The big picture
- ✳ Living in hotels
- ✳ Boredom
- ✳ Phoning home
- ✳ Dos and don'ts guide to surviving life on the road

What the pros take on tour

❝ I used to take a sunlamp. Much to the others' hysteria I used to sit on the bog with this sunlamp. ❞
Paul McCartney (Q Magazine).

How to survive irritating band members and road personnel

It's becoming more common place these days for artists and bands to go on tour with their own masseurs, chefs and fitness coaches. Sooner or later it will surprise no one if every tour hires their own resident psychiatrist to help musicians and road crew deal with the stresses and strains that living out of a suitcase can create. Even if you are travelling with your regular band and you all get along famously in normal circumstances, when you are forced to be in each other's company 18 hours a day, conflicts can crop up which even a healthy sized sense of humour can find hard to reach. Tiredness goes a long way towards turning usually affable personalities into psychotic neurotics.

6 One of the things I have learned, which is really strange, about being on the road is that everybody tends to go out on the road, and sort of go berserk – especially the first times they've been out. One of the best things you can do is sleep and eat well, would you believe? What ends up happening is that within a really short period of time, no matter what you're doing – it's very difficult to deal with things if you're not sleeping well. One of the things I've definitely done ... on planes and tour buses I've always just tried to sleep as much as is humanly possible. It actually takes the edge off and makes your days go a lot quicker.9
Bobby Messano (guitar: Steve Winwood, Robin Beck).

6 I fell asleep on stage one time, midway through 'Fool To Cry,' I think. Hey, it's a slow song man.9
Keith Richards talking to Alan Grice (Encore Magazine).

Even if you are on a big tour and staying in luxury hotels, touring becomes exhausting in a very short space of time. The success of a tour has as much to do with how well each road member copes with performing in a different country every night; the relentless checking in and out of hotels; the constant packing and unpacking; and how each tour member gets on with each other, as it does your ability to put on a great show.

6 It's a surrogate family thrown together at random, and some are more dysfunctional than others.9
Julie Homi (keyboards: Robert Palmer, Yanni, Peter Cetera).

There is a saying that every oyster needs a pinch of grit (irritation) before it can make a pearl. In musician terms this can be interpreted to mean, every tour has it's pain in the ass who has to be endured before the group can put on a great show. This is the person (hopefully there will be only one – although on some tours there can be more) who irritates the rest of the crew so much that they have to constantly fight the compulsion to

Advice clinic with Julie Homi

Q How do you cope with living at such close quarters to other band members?

A This isn't a problem for me, as long as I have my own hotel room, and can have privacy when I need it. I think you have to be sociable to be happy on the road, because you are around people a lot, and you are meeting strangers every day. I like getting on the bus after a show, eating pizza, joking about something funny that happened that night, maybe playing a game or watching a video. It's like a pyjama party.' *Julie Homi (keyboards: Robert Palmer, Yanni, Peter Cetera).*

gag the offender with gaffer tape, wrap them in cling film and superglue them to the ceiling of their hotel room.

Usually what happens to these people is that on the last day of the tour they get gagged with gaffer tape, wrapped in cling film and superglued to the ceiling of their hotel room.

Advice clinic with Bobby Messano

Q Does every tour have its own pain in the butt?

A Absolutely, and you usually turn to your road manager or your tour manager and say 'please – I can't take this person,' and let them take care of it. It's very strange, especially being thrown into a situation with people you don't know at all, and you have to cultivate relationships rather quickly.

How do you deal with the grit of the tour?

Keeping a sense of humour about all the niggly problems and personality clashes which sometimes happen during a tour can go a long way in preventing ugly outbursts and bad atmospheres. Humour is an excellent tool to defuse potentially volatile situations. If you are experiencing a sense of humour failure try and get as far away from the problem zone as possible. And if that is not enough find a way to let off steam. Hard physical exercise usually works well and can be done wherever you are no matter how little spare time you have in your schedule. If you have more time though, getting out and sightseeing, or shopping, or going to the movies can give you just the kind of time out you need for your sense of humour to return.

What do you do if you discover that it's you who has been voted the pain of the tour?

If more than one person is finding it hard being near you you should listen to what they have to say. The most annoying people to deal with for long periods of time are those who are loud and obnoxious, those who moan all the time, tend to be selfish or have other irritating traits such as being constantly late for pick-ups, soundchecks etc. If you fall into any or all of these categories you need to find a way to relax more.

If there are things you do which you know bug other people try not to do them. At the same time don't become defensive. If your fellow band members have all agreed that you are irritating the heck out of them don't get hostile about it, even if you think you have good reason for your behaviour. Once they have made their points let it go and concentrate on what you need to do to turn the situation around.

> 'Respecting others (including your band mates) would be my main bit of advice. Don't let egos and bad attitudes come into play, you may find yourself being sent back home on the bus alone and replaced in the middle of the tour. Remember, the tour group will be your extended family for a week, month, or even longer. So there's no room for bad vibes. And be on time. It's a drag waiting around for people that have no consideration for other peoples' time and are always late. I don't care how great a player you are, if you get a bad reputation for always being late, you're gonna stop getting called for gigs.'
> *Gene Williams (keyboards: tours: Roberta Flack, Chaka Khan, Joe).*

> 'Get to know your band and crew mates. Many are actually great people despite that fact they have chosen to run away and join the circus for a living.'
> *Kevin Dukes (guitar: Boz Scaggs, Don Henley, Jackson Browne).*

Letting off steam

> 'Believe it or not – the road gets very boring. There is so much waiting and sitting around you can let it get to you. It can very easily cause you to turn dark about your situation. At first we just drank a lot – go out trying to meet girls. Sure we still do that but I seem to drink less. Exercise – even a little, –

get out of the room. More often than not you will find yourself watching 'Spies Like Us' every weekend out on the road. The television is a powerful thing in that hotel room. There is a lot of great programming out there now but on the road you may often find you turn towards the junk or things you have seen countless times – probably the comfort of familiarity. Go for a walk or something. I work out a lot at home so I try to continue it on the road. I carry a bag with my in-line skates during the summer – great way to see a place and get some exercise.
Billy Hulting (percussion: Lou Rawls, Natalie Cole, Barry Manilow, Maynard Ferguson).

Any activity which is far removed from the day to day routine of touring life will help you stay sane on the road. Sports work well because they can help you burn off excess energy. Portable hobbies such as photography and reading can work just as well. Musicians, being the creative folks they are, will often find unusual and inventive ways to pass the time.

Every tour I've done has its own store of private jokes, and I try to contribute as much as I can. I like getting to the point where I'm laughing so hard, I'm afraid I might have an accident. It reminds me of summer camp. Some tours have a newsletter, which usually has a humorous bent, and I like to contribute to those, too. I have shot comedy videos about the tour. This was a great creative outlet for me, and a source of entertainment and embarrassment for others. One video became so ambitious, I missed a soundcheck once because I was filming a scene. I don't recommend that. I call friends at home regularly. Life on the road can get very insular, and it is important to remind myself that I have another life waiting for me when the tour ends.
Julie Homi (keyboards: Peter Cetera, Yanni, Robert Palmer).

What the pros take on tour

Movies, books, magazines, laptops, games. I try not to take too much stuff with me these days ... it's a drag moving it all around. Traveling light is the way to go. We all share everything, so it's all good.
Gene Williams (keyboards: tours: Roberta Flack, Chaka Khan, Joe).

Going solo

If you are a solo musician you will be spared the ego conflicts of travelling groups but instead will have to deal with boredom and sometimes the loneliness of extended trips abroad. This can be particularly daunting when you are in a country where you don't speak the language. There is rarely a problem which does not also present a benefit though. During breaks and off-duty periods find out from the staff and the locals where the interesting places to go are. Often they will be pleased to show you around. If you don't speak the language there is no better time to start learning – especially if your contract is for a month or more. You may even find people who want to learn your language, particularly if your first language happens to be English. If you are touring around Asia and look as though you speak English it is highly likely that at some point you will be stopped in the street by a student who will pull out their text books and ask you to help them with their homework. It can be a novel way to spend an afternoon, and for some it can become a lucrative side-line.

What the pros take on tour

'I travel really lightly. On the bigger tours people take all kinds of stuff, and actually some of the guys in my band will take golf clubs with them. We're going to Park City Utah for the World Cup Skiing and everybody in the band ... I think everybody but me skis, so they'll have their ski gear with them, but for me I like to travel really light. I think music's really important. You'll be on the road and most everybody has a portable cassette or CD player with headphones that they can use on the plane and in their room. And I'll take some books.'

Tim Scott (bass: Tower of Power, Stevie Wonder).

Advice clinic by Billy Hulting

Q What are the bad bits about touring?

A There are quite a few – early leave times from hotels, bad rental gear, two shows in one day separated by three hours, bad information from hotel employees, screaming babies on planes, late flights, screaming babies on delayed flights after an early leave, not being at home. There are all sorts of quirky weird things to deal with *but* – the way to stay sane is to realize you are making a living playing an instrument – *playing* is the key word here. Maynard Ferguson used to say 'I never went to work a day in my life – I always went to play.' If you believe in luck – you are lucky to not only be playing but lucky that you landed a tour.' Billy Hulting (percussion: Lou Rawls, Natalie Cole, Barry Manilow, Maynard Ferguson).

What to expect

Knowing what to expect on a tour can go a long way to help you deal with whatever touring life can throw at you. Sometimes it manages to throw quite a lot.

' Worst-funniest-memorable moment? Getting arrested and thrown in jail for being too young while playing in a club in Oklahoma; accidentally letting a crazed audience member grab my guitar and having it all start a riot where people got hurt and I could have been sued; the end of a tour when the crew and band give each other some big surprises – such as the crew dropping hundreds of fish from above the stage onto the band; playing in your hometown with all of your old friends and family there to cheer you on. I could go on and on. '
Dawayne Bailey (guitar: Bob Seger, Chicago).

Travel complications are a common topic when it comes to tour memories of the less pleasant kind.

' The worst about the road is whatever airline scheduling hell you go through, and it can happen anytime. Sitting on a plane or in an airport longer than you need to is always hell. A hellish example was finishing a show in Saint Petersburg Russia at 11:00 pm, staying up in a band suite with everyone on the tour until the bus departure for the airport at 5:00 am. Flying from St. Pete at 7am to Moscow, holding over until noon to fly to London. Arriving in London expecting a two hour layover that increased hour by hour into a twelve hour lay over. Finally getting into LA eleven hours later to find they had lost my luggage. Welcome home. '
Kevin Dukes (guitar: Boz Scaggs, Don Henley, Jackson Browne).

Of all the rules of the road though, most musicians find that whatever bad stuff happens to them, sooner or later there will be equal good stuff as compensation.

' Some of the concert halls I've soloed in – Suntory Hall in Japan, Philharmonic Hall in Berlin in front of twenty million TV viewers at the Berlin Jazz Festival – they were great. Meeting and hanging with some great players after a gig we shared the bill on. '
Billy Hulting (percussion: Lou Rawls, Natalie Cole, Barry Manilow, Maynard Ferguson).

' The best thing is not particularly any one thing. I've met the President, played some very important musical and social events like the first Farm Aid, several Amnesty International

Festivals in the States and abroad, saw Russia before the fall of communism and have gotten to see much of the world and met people I would not have had the opportunity to do in many other lines of work. That I would say is the best part of it; the unique opportunities touring offers – to see the world in a way few ever have the chance to.

Kevin Dukes (guitar: Boz Scaggs, Don Henley, Jackson Browne).

The big picture

'Life on the road is full of paradoxes. It's complicated, because a large group of people are mounting a sophisticated production in a different town almost every night, yet it's simple, because as a band member, all I have to do is be in the hotel lobby when the tour manager tells me to. Everything else is taken care of. I am transported, fed, provided with a place to sleep at night and a wake-up call in the morning. My luggage is carried for me, my gear is set-up on stage. Life on the road can be lonely, especially on a long tour, but it can be very social, also a great opportunity to hook up with good friends I hardly ever see, make new friends, or even live out my fantasies with musical admirers (that's politically correct for groupies). A strong connection can develop with others in the group, and sometimes lasting friendships are formed.

When a good tour ends, my feelings are bittersweet. I'm ready to go home, yet there is regret about leaving the group, who have come to feel like my family. The road is tedious and predictable, yet full of surprises. It's glamorous one minute and uncomfortable the next. You can be the toast of the town one place and unable to fill the house in another.

Julie Homi (keyboards: Peter Cetera, Yanni, Robert Palmer)

Living in hotels

What the pros take on tour

'When I go on tour I tend to take no clothing and lots of books. I'm more of a reader than a listener.

Jewel (Q Magazine).

You don't have to be on the road long before every hotel room starts to look suspiciously like the one you just checked-out from. After a couple of weeks the sameness only adds to your disorientation and you'll find yourself taping reminder notes to the mirror so that when you wake up you'll know which country/state/city you are in. Better quality hotels are a mixed blessing. Along with the fluffy towels come a selection of expensive temptations.

Mini bars

A stroke of genius by the hotel marketing department. There is probably no traveller left on this planet who hasn't stayed over-night in a great hotel room and experienced post mini-bar remorse the following morning. Yes, you know that you'll be charged ten times the retail price but it's there, and at three o'clock in the morning when your body clock thinks it's mid-afternoon, £6 for a beer or a bar of chocolate seems perfectly reasonable. The biggest problem comes for those who manage to empty their mini-bars overnight. Be warned, the starting price for an emptied mini-bar can be around £80. That can put a real dent in your per diems!

' Trying to explain to a hotel person who didn't speak much English that, in my opinion, my previous night's mini-bar bill would, in one fell swoop, solve their national debt, was always tricky. '
Martin Jenner (guitar: Cliff Richard, Everly Brothers) on cultural problems.

Laundry

This can be a tricky one because in many hotels the in-house laundry service is reasonably priced and as a result it's easy to get lulled into the habit of using the hotel service without checking the fees. In some hotels though you will be able to go out and buy replacement clothes cheaper than it would cost to get them washed and ironed. Unless you don't need to keep within a specific budget it's worthwhile checking.

It's also worth bearing in mind that although some hotels identify your clothes by placing an adhesive sticker displaying your room number on them, some use permanent ink marker pens. If you are fastidious about your clothes it can be upsetting having your favourite designer garment returned with a serial number inked into the collar, cuff or waistband. Similarly, if you have a favourite outfit which you would be upset about never seeing again, or seeing it shrunk, or with an iron shine, wash it by hand yourself as the laundry service can be quite brutal on clothes, and they usually offer little or no compensation for lost or damaged clothing.

Telephones

The cost of making phone calls from your hotel room is loaded by about 500%. Without an international phone company credit card (such as MCI or AT&T) you can easily eat up vast chunks of your tour earnings on phone calls alone (see phoning home section later in this chapter).

> 6 The only thing that really annoys me in hotels is making phone calls because if you don't have some kind of phone credit card then they're gonna harass you with taxes. 9
> *Bobby Messano (guitar: Steve Winwood, Robin Beck).*

On the plus side, the better quality hotels will tend to have their own gym, swimming pool, or squash courts etc. which not only are great places to visit when you have an hour or so to kill but also help you burn off road stress, and help keep you in reasonable shape.

What the pros take on tour

> 6 To make synthetic filled hotel rooms a bit more hospitable I've carried around a humidifier (hotel rooms can be notoriously dry) Incense, big scarfs to drape over glaring hotel lamps (make sure they're not going to get hot and catch on fire!), and a citrus spray you get at health food stores that when sprayed in a room, not only smells nice, but attaches itself to synthetic particles and negative ions and helps to eliminate them from the stuffy room air. 9
> *Susie Davis (keyboards: Billy Idol, Sinead O'Connor, Van Morrison).*

On some tours, especially if you are an upcoming act or support act you may find yourself having to share your hotel room with a fellow band member. Even the most easy going musicians will find this difficult, even for short periods, and it is a situation which can pose problems far greater than deciding who gets custody of the TV remote control.

> 6 I try not to do that any more. I don't really have to as a rule. The best thing is to pick out the person that you like the most, that you think you're gonna get along with the best. If you get stuck with someone you don't like you'd better buy yourself some handcuffs. There's usually a kind of natural pairing off system, where people gravitate towards each other. You need a lot of patience and tolerance and acceptance of people's behaviour, – of their habits. 9
> *Tim J. Scott (bass: Stevie Wonder, Tower of Power).*

' In my case, in the Santana band, most of us have known each other awhile, and we're all pretty good friends. If it's a case where you're just thrown together with a bunch of other people you don't know, then it becomes an exercise in learning to get along with strangers. Eventually you find the common ground between everybody, and you can interact with them on those levels. It's just like the rest of life – everybody's different, so cut each other some slack, okay? Make a little extra effort to understand the other person's ways. '
Benny Rietveld (bass: Santana, Sheila E, Miles Davis).

What the pros take on tour

' At one point I played golf regularly. Now I have a road case for my mountain bike and I have seen places I've been dozens of times in a completely new light, plus have the added benefit of being able to exercise outdoors and burn off road steam. I have taken pillows, recording gear, golf clubs, books, but now it's primarily my bike. '
Kevin Dukes (guitar: Boz Scaggs, Don Henley, Jackson Browne).

If you are sharing a room it helps to give each other as much privacy as possible. If you both like to have your own space aim to give each other some time to be alone there each day. Just going out to explore the hotel, going for a swim or hanging out in the bar or the cafe for an hour can make all the difference and can go a long way to help stave off 'road claustrophobia.'

What is most likely to annoy you about living in hotels?
The actual process of living in hotels can become irritating in itself – especially if you value your privacy. The better the tour you are on the better the hotels, and strangely enough the less privacy you have. There will be times when you'll swear more

Advice clinic with Carol Kaye

Q How do you deal with living at such close quarters with fellow band members?

A Keep your own space, even if it's just part of a hotel room; respect others and they usually respect you but don't be a 'pushover' out of 'kindness' – everyone should pull their own weight, keep a good sense of humor, yet be quiet a lot of the times too.
Carol Kaye (bass: Hampton Hawes).

people pass through your hotel room in a day than Piccadilly Circus in a week. First there will be housekeeping, then the mini bar attendant, the laundry, then the person who turns down your bed, then the person to replace your towels, – it is difficult to relax in those circumstances, and the Do Not Disturb notice is not much of a defence. Put that out on your door handle and you'll often have a string of phone calls instead from members of each department telling you they need to get into your room.

What are the best bits about living in hotels?

Having everything done for you is one of the huge bonuses of hotel living. You don't have to do anything other than get up at some point in the day and go to work. The rest is taken care of.

> I don't have to make the bed ... I don't have to clean up. I don't live like a pig in hotels either, 'cos I don't like to, but it's pretty cool that you don't have to clean up.
> *Tim J. Scott (bass: Stevie Wonder, Tower of Power).*

What the pros take on tour

> CD Player and a Cassette deck. Some of the tours I've been on they set up a little room with a four-track or eight-track if you felt like writing, or something, which was sort of neat. I always have a micro cassette recorder. I write a lot. I'll always have that with me so I can write something real quick and throw it on a micro cassette.
> *Bobby Messano (guitar: Steve Winwood, Robin Beck).*

Boredom

If genetic scientists one day discover that musicians have a gene which causes not only a low boredom threshold but is also responsible for them being able to think up wildly creative and reckless ways to relieve the boredom, tour managers, for one, won't be surprised. For many touring bands the hotel becomes their playground. Sometimes it's an expensive one, too.

> We had a $68,000 bill in Australia one time. I used to carry the receipt around as a joke. *Jon Bon Jovi (Empire Magazine).*

There's nothing like a tour for encouraging band members to regress back to to less than adult behaviour.

> Everyone collected the large bags provided by hotels for dirty laundry, and we saved them until we were in a tall hotel. The

person with the highest room would be the host. The laundry bags would be filled with water and ceremoniously hurled out of the window onto the car park below. Forty odd litres of water travelling at 64 feet per second! While there were many funny nights at this a couple in particular spring to mind. In Brussels a 'bombing' raid from the 32nd floor took place with us blissfully unaware that the joint Chiefs of Staff of several countries were having a NATO summit nearby and that the sonic results of our activities were causing much consternation among the troops guarding their hotel. Amazingly nothing was said. The final blow came when we accidentally side-swiped a rental van one night. That was another bill. After that the band and crew were never booked into rooms higher than the second floor.
Martin Jenner (guitar: Cliff Richard, Everly Brothers).

I've had a few jokes played on me. It usually involves ruining the bed that you plan on sleeping in. Someone poured beer into my bed once. It was soggy and it smelled bad. I've also had some shaving cream put in my bed and once I actually had someone take some cheese and jam it into the lock on my hotel room door and so I couldn't get in.
Tim J. Scott (bass: Stevie Wonder, Tower of Power).

Some pranks have a sense of artistry that one suspects even Leonardo De Vinci would have been proud of.

The lifts had to be targeted as they contained irresistible magnets in the form of exquisitely shot photos. Usually at around 4:00 am someone would enter the lifts, remove the photos and after some inventive alterations they would be returned. Some while later early morning guests were treated to a smiling chef holding his culinary creation in which would be various parts of the human anatomy culled from assorted 'health' magazines, while the swimming pool photo would show bronzed, bathing beauties with Roger Whittaker's and Frank Ifield's heads superimposed. Smiling skiers would descend the local ski-slopes with large exposed breasts flying in the wind regardless of their gender.

Most hotels would remove the pictures and nothing would be said but one Hotel in Denmark took a dim view and presented us with a bill of huge proportions. That was when the word from above came that that particular method of recreation would have to cease. It did.
Mart Jenner (guitar: Cliff Richard, Everly Brothers).

Phoning home

What ET went through to phone home is nothing compared to
what the average traveller has to endure if they are abroad
without a phone company credit card.

Phone company credit card

By far the cheapest way to call home other than a 1–800 or
Friends and Family number (which you can use for long distance
calls in your home country).

> I don't make long phone calls but we'd touch base every few
> days, and talk for a few minutes and it depends, if I'm in
> Europe I probably don't call quite as often as I would if we
> were in the States, and I'd try to call at a reasonable hour. I
> have a 1–800 number at home. If I'm in the States I can call
> that number and it's a cheaper rate than say, using a calling
> card or something like that.
> *Steve Howard (horns: Paul McCartney, Ray Charles, Albert
> Collins).*

Using your calling card you can charge the call to your home
phone. Many hotels levy a surcharge for using their telephone
network though.

> I use a calling card and charge all my long distance calls to my
> home phone. Some hotels don't charge a surcharge still but if
> they do it's fairly nominal ... and so I just get the one bill at
> my house.
> *Tim J. Scott (bass: Stevie Wonder, Tower of Power).*

Phone cards

Depending on where in the world you are these are either easy to
use or require a certain amount of patience. The easy countries
are the ones which offer only one phone card. Phone cards are
typically sold in newsagents and local stores and can be bought
in several different values (usually anything from £5 to £10, or
$10 – $20 depending on the local currency), and can be used at
any payphone which accepts cards. To use them all you have to
do is put the card in the machine, dial the number you want and
you are through.

In countries where there is more than one phone card
company operating you may need to follow the instructions on
the back of the card. This usually entails punching in a fifteen
digit security number and following a sequence of voice prompts.
The drawback to this type of card is that you have to go through

✳ TIP ✳

Just as each telephone company has pluses and minuses when it comes to the service they offer, phone card companies are the same. If you are going to be using them a lot it will be worthwhile making a few enquiries to find out which company currently offers the best deal. It's also worthwhile remembering that some of the phone card companies will charge you for a call (at the minimum call rate) even if you don't get through. Those are the cards to be avoided.

✳ TIP ✳

Every road musician has off days – especially if they have left partners and family behind, but if you reach a point when you are desperate to talk to loved ones, it is best to avoid doing so at all costs. Making a call at that moment will only emphasise the distance between you and make you miss them more. By the time you hang up you will probably be feeling even more homesick then before you made the call. As hard as it seems, at times like that it is better to put off phoning home until you feel less needful.

this extended procedure each time you use it. The plus side to it is that once it has run out you can use your credit card to buy more time for it instead of having to buy another card.

Phone cards are still an expensive way to make a phone call compared to the kind of rate you would get from your home phone, but using them is cheaper than phoning from your hotel room.

> ❛ I love the telephone. The longest call I made was for six hours, including bathroom breaks, from Atlanta to my girlfriend in LA. ❜ *KD Lang (Q Magazine).*

Credit cards

In some countries you can use your credit card like a regular phone card and get a similar rate. In others you will be routed through a long distance carrier and will probably get a rate which is not as good as that offered by one of the phone cards. If you are going through a long distance carrier ask them what their rate is before making the call. It could save you from a shock when your credit card bill comes in.

Coins

If you are in a country which accepts large denomination coins in their payphones (like Britain), it is easy to make an international call with coins, and just a matter of putting in the money and dialing the number. In somewhere like the US though it isn't a reasonable option unless you have nothing else to do for half an hour and you enjoy humiliation. You will need to have about $12 in quarters on standby for the minimum call and after having fed the machine 48 coins and being ridiculed by the operator for not having a phone credit card ('what third world country are you from then?') you'll probably go straight out and buy the phone card you should have bought earlier because it's far cheaper anyway.

Telephone office

In some countries you can go into a local telephone or telegraph office and make your calls from there. The rate you get will be better or similar to the payphone rate but the surroundings are usually a bit more comfortable and offer you a better degree of privacy.

> ❛ I don't know – thousands of dollars in phone calls? ❜
> Bobby Messano *(guitar: Steve Winwood, Robin Beck)* on ways to keep sane while on the road.

Dos and don'ts guide to surviving the road

There are two ways to go on tour. One is the hard way and the other is the slightly less hard way.

Advice clinic with Julie Homi

Q What advice would you give to anyone going on tour for the first time?

A 1 Be considerate of the crew, not demanding. Remember that however exhausted you may feel on the road, they work much longer, harder hours and probably feel ten times worse.
2 Avoid becoming romantically or sexually involved with anyone in the organization. This is much easier said than done. The road can be a lonely place, and most of us want to cuddle up with someone at the end of the night. However, it is far safer to make new friends along the way (or fly old ones in) than to complicate your professional life with personal entanglements.'
3 Don't complain too much, especially at first. If you do complain, try and do it with a sense of humor. It will be better received.'

What the pros take on tour

'I carry a Mac Powerbook with me so I can be very productive. I can stay in touch with friends via e-mail, work with Finale to get charts ready, ear training, type letters. I even learned how to design a web page while riding in a van on the way to a gig.'
Billy Hulting (percussion: Lou Rawls, Natalie Cole, Barry Manilow, Maynard Ferguson).

7
Making the most of your opportunities on the road

The success of any tour depends as much upon how efficient the promotion team is as it does the band's or artist's ability to deliver the goods on stage. You may be brilliant performers but if you have an overstretched or badly organised promotion department which hasn't been able to get that information across to the media, you'll be playing to empty halls. This is not just a problem for the new and upcoming acts either, many successful and established entertainers share the same difficulties. Record companies have limited resources and have to juggle the interests of dozens of acts. Hardly ever will an act receive as much promotional support as they would like. The more each act can do for themselves the more successful the tour will be irrespective of whether you are a band setting out on a college tour for the first time or you have already sold 15 million albums and are supporting the Rolling Stones on their World

Tour. There is no such thing as too much promotion.

If you don't have record company or management support have a band meeting to work out your own promotion strategy. It is far less daunting than it may at first appear.

Getting the word out

The aim of every promotion campaign or strategy is to let the world know you are out there and that you are worthy of their attention. Before you can create a plan you need to ask yourself three questions.

1 What do you want to achieve?
2 How big an area do you want the promotion to cover?
3 How much can you afford to spend?

What do you want to achieve?
The answer to this will depend on what stage of development you are in. If you are a new band your goal might just be to get more people coming to your local gigs. Later on, once you have an established fan base you will probably want to target a larger audience and be wanting to promote a CD release. Later still you will be considering your long term prospects within the music industry.

How big an area do you want the promotion to cover?
This may be anything from your local neighbourhood, city, state, or country to territories overseas.

How much can you afford to spend?
Obviously £200 is not going to enable you to strike a worldwide campaign, but it is surprising how much can be accomplished on even the smallest of budgets. Once you know how much you have available to you, you will be able to plan accordingly.

The publicity machine

The key to the success of any promotional campaign is creativity. It doesn't matter which part of the media or the public you are targeting if whatever you do catches their attention you are more than half way to achieving a satisfactory return for your effort. Newspapers, magazines, TV and radio all have an insatiable appetite for news and information and there are more and more of them every day. So with an inexhaustible supply of media outlets seeking ways to fill their pages and time slots all you have to do is give them something they can use.

TIP

If you have a record company or a manager that will be devising a publicity campaign for you, it is worth while discussing their plans with them as early as you can. The more you know about what is being arranged for you the more prepared you will be.

The promotional tools

Fliers and posters

For many bands and artists this is the first advertising tool they will use. It is an easy and effective way to promote your next gig or special event. Anyone who has access to a computer can create a professional looking poster/flier at an extremely low cost. Even if you don't have a computer most people will know someone who does and who can be talked into helping the band put one together.

✳ **TIP** ✳
Recruit people to hand out fliers in shopping malls.

Distribution

Make sure the venue you will be performing in has a supply of your promotional material at least a couple of weeks before you are due to appear. Before distributing elsewhere decide who your target audience is. If you are a jazz band there's probably little point in promoting your gig at the local University (unless the university is renowned for its appreciation of jazz). If you are a band with student appeal though it is exactly the right place to have posters and fliers on display.

Local press

Every newspaper has a local entertainment news section. Most will include a local Gig Guide or a What's On type of column which lists up and coming events. If the venue you are playing doesn't already promote their gig calendar there phone up the newspaper and give them the info yourself. You might even find yourself put through to the writer and at the same time be able to ask him (or her) what type of stories/features they are interested in. Is there something newsworthy about your gig? Give it some thought and there's bound to be an interesting angle to be found.

Maybe you've just competed in a Battle of the Bands contest; or you are performing as part of a fund raising event; or your lead singer has a reputation for diving off the speaker cabinets; or the last time you played your guitarist was nearly electrocuted – anything that will grab the attention of the columnist and the readers alike.

Press release

Writing press releases and distributing them to the media is a habit worth cultivating. It is effective and cheap. Many people mistakingly feel that writing a release requires journalistic skills but although having a flair for writing is an advantage it is by no means a necessity and is a skill anyone can learn. There are also plenty of books available to guide you through the process (check out the guide books for writers section in your local book store).

Essentially a press release should convey five pieces of information:

1 What is the news?
2 Who is making the news?
3 Where is it happening?
4 When is it happening?
5 Why is it happening?

Keep your press release short and to the point. Any information which does not answer any of the five questions listed above should be left out. Bear in mind that newspapers receive hundreds of press releases every day so make yours newsworthy.

Your press release should be mailed or delivered to the newspaper and accompanied by a photo whenever possible. Some newspapers will also agree to receive press releases via fax or e-mail but you should ask them first as some editors and sub editors prefer not to.

Sample press release – and don't forget to include a photo of the band

PRESS RELEASE
September 30th 1998

Rising Up From The Dead ... 1

Pop group, Dead Ahead have rescheduled their cancelled performance at the Blah Blah Club. Two weeks ago their show came to an unexpected halt when lead guitarist, Matt Hurt was almost electrocuted due to a faulty earth connection beneath the stage. The guitarist was taken to hospital and treated for minor burns but has since made a good recovery.

'I don't remember what happened, to be honest,' Hurt said of the accident, 'but I'm fine now and looking forward to doing the gig.'

Dead Ahead will be appearing at the Blah Blah Club on October 10th. Doors open at 8:30pm. Tickets are £7 and will be available through the venue's box office.

The performance is part of the band's eight week tour to promote the release of their new CD 'Volts A-Go Go.'

Ends ...

Enquiries about this release should be made to Chris Evers, Band PR on Tel: 0171-000-000.

TIP

Keep copies of all the newspaper articles and columns you are featured in. They could be worth showing potential sponsors later on (see later section on Sponsorship).

Fan database

Once you begin to develop a following you can get to work on your fan database. Invite your fans to sign up for your band mailing list so that you will be able to keep them up to date on your performing schedule and any other noteworthy news and events you may have. Getting this started is as easy as taking along a stack of postcard sized invitations to gigs and making them available to people at the door. Making the invitation as creative, friendly or as humourous as you can will encourage people to sign up.

Sample band mailing list invitation

Dead Ahead mailing list

Do you wanna join the family?
Sign up to join our free hotline service and be sure never to miss one of our gigs again!

Name _____

Address _____

_____

State/County _____

Zip/Postcode _____

See ya at the next gig!

TIP

Mailing lists can expand at a rapid rate causing your mailing costs to rise at equal speed. To cover all or part of the costs see if you can recruit a local company or venue to buy a block of advertising space in your newsletter or to sponsor you. Your local musical instrument store, record or clothing shop could be good starting places (see Sponsorship later in this chapter).

Newsletter

Once your mailing list is established your next task will be to make use of it. Creating a newsletter can be time consuming but it is also an effective way of reminding the world that you are out there, and can be an interesting project to put together. The most vital piece of information in it will probably be your gig schedule. You will want everyone to know when and where your next gig or gigs are going to be for them to come and see you. The rest is up to you.

Newsletters can be as simple or as complex as you want them to be. You might just decide to mail out your flier. Then again you might decide that a full blown newsletter will be a good way to tell your fans all about your last tour; or special event; give them more information about the band members; or will enable you to tell them about the video or CD you're making.

Radio/TV

Radio and TV stations can be surprisingly receptive to
approaches from even the newest of bands and artists if they can
see the potential for a story. Send them your press release as
well. Your guitarist's almost electrocution (or any other event)
could provide them with just the type of filler they need to
round-off a local news bulletin and at the same time give you
and the band excellent publicity. If nothing headline grabbing is
happening within the band, think of ways to make yourselves
topical. Performing a benefit; inviting a famous guest to the
show; playing a free gig in the park etc., could be ways to drum
up some free promotion.

Find out if the radio station in the area you are going to be
gigging in is interested in interviewing you. If you are in your
home town it could be that they have a special interest in
promoting local talent. If you are from out of town the angle of
an upcoming or already established band will be just as useful.
Find out which DJ is likely to be the most interested. Invite him
or her to the gig and offer them free tickets to give away to their
listeners. Send them your promotion pack and if you have a
single or CD to promote make sure they have a copy.

The World Wide Web

With each day bringing hundreds of new users to the World
Wide Web it is only a question of time before it will be
recognised as the promotional tool of the era. Getting the
information onto the Web is simple, but getting it on in such a
way that it becomes immediately accessible to your target
audience will be the difference between promotional success or
failure. If no one knows you exist they are not going to be
looking for you on the Web, but if you already have a name or
sign up with a website which has an established network of
visitors the potential is there for the word to get around and the
rest will be up to you.

How do I promote myself on the World Wide Web?

If you are not yet an established act take a look at the websites
which promote new bands, musicians and artists. A search
under Musicians Directories or Musicians Services will reveal
hundreds of them. Some of them (especially if they are new sites)
even offer free listings.

A good site should offer you enough space to list a bio,
photographs and offer sound bytes of your material. Most sites

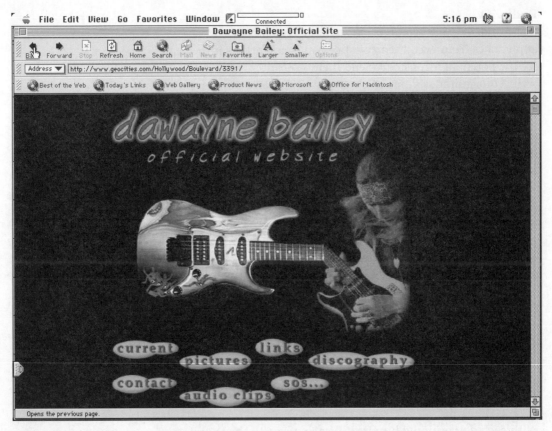

 File Edit View Go Favorites Window 🖵 ▭ Connected 5:16 pm 🌀 ② 🌐

Dawayne Bailey: Official Site

Back Forward Stop Refresh Home Search Mail News Favorites Larger Smaller Options

Address ▼ http://www.geocities.com/Hollywood/Boulevard/3391/

Best of the Web Today's Links Web Gallery Product News Microsoft Office for Macintosh

dawayne bailey
official website

current   links
pictures   discography
contact   sos...
audio clips

Opens the previous page.

Dawayne Bailey's site is at http://www.geocities.com/Hollywood/Boulevard/3391

also display a visitor's page which will tell you how many hits (visitors) the site has had, which will give you an indication of how successful their marketing is.

Established acts will either develop their own site or be featured on their record company's website, or both. As some record companies only offer fairly basic information about each of their signings on their website, many bands and artists decide to set up their own domain as well, and link the two together. This means that anyone visiting the record company site can connect directly to the band's or artist's own pages with a click of the mouse.

Web sites of some of the musicians featured in this book
On this page and over the next few we show you some of the web sites set up by musicians featured in this book. Look and learn!

File Edit View Go Favorites Window	Connected	5:07 pm

The Official Carol Kaye Web Site

Refresh Home Search Mail News Favorites Larger Smaller Options

Address ▼ | http://www.carolkaye.com/

Best of the Web   Today's Links   Web Gallery   Product News   Microsoft   Office for Macintosh

Carol Kaye

If you have listened to the radio or watched TV in the past 35 years, you've heard her play.

Carol was one of the core group of anonymous studio musicians who lent her unique styles of studio Guitar and Electric Bass playing to many of the hits recorded by such popular artists like the Beach Boys, Ray Charles, The Righteous Bros., Johnny Mathis, Nancy Sinatra, Sam Cooke, Glen Campbell, Lou Rawls, Jan & Dean, Henry Mancini, The Lettermen, Paul Revere & Raiders, Monkees, Buckinghams, April & Nino, Sonny & Cher, Chris Montez, Andy Williams, Quincy Jones, Joe Cocker, Ike & Tina Turner, Mel Torme, Bobby Darin, Frank Zappa, Wayne Newton, Herb Alpert, O.C. Smith, Don Ho, Al Martino, and a few Motown (LA).

Numerous movie and TV credits including MASH, Mission Impossible, Brady Bunch, Addams Family, Cannon, McCloud, Room 222, 1st Bill Cosby, Ironside, Kojak, Hawaii 5-O, Wonder Woman, Soap; Thomas Crown Affair, Sweet Charity, Airport, In The Heat Of The Night, Plaza Suite, The New Centurions, Pawnbroker, Guess Who's Coming To Dinner, Change Of Habit, Le Mans, Walk Don't Run to name a few.

biography

Networking

Once you get out on the road it is amazing not only how many people you get to meet but also how many of those turn out to be useful and potentially influential contacts. Songwriter Jimmy Scott once found himself sitting next to singer Phyllis Nelson's manager on a plane. That chance meeting led to Nelson recording one of Scott's songs on her next album. You never can tell who you might meet so it is worthwhile always having some contact information close to hand – even if it is just a business card.

Drop in on Carol Kaye at
http://www.carolkaye.com

The six people theory

Script consultant Linda Seger once spoke in a lecture of the theory that everyone is connected to everyone else on this planet by six people. What this means in practice is, say for example you wanted to be able to get a CD or demo to Muff Winwood, there will be someone you know, who will know somebody, who will know somebody else, who in turn will know somebody, who knows somebody else who knows someone who can get that CD or demo to Muff Winwood. The key to making

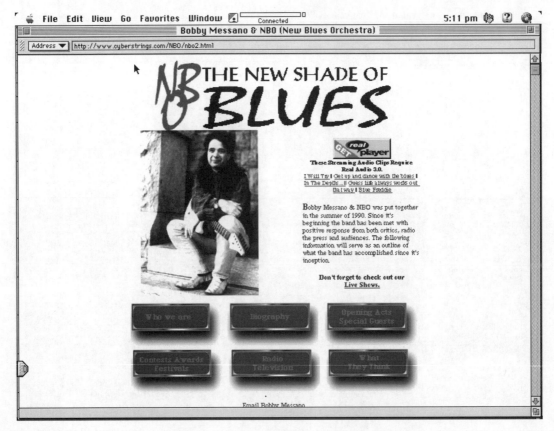

Bobby Messano's site at
http://www.messano.com

it happen is successful networking. If you can't do it you need to develop your network more, speak to people about what you do and what you want to achieve. When they refer you to someone follow up on it. Treat everything as a lead.

Develop your black book of contacts

Once you've made the contacts don't let them go to waste. At the very least make sure the information is stored in an address book or electronic organiser for later use. Besides their name and contact numbers, write down notes to remind yourself where you met and what they do. On tour when you are meeting people all the time this type of information is easy to forget.

* TIP *

Great contacts should be nurtured – invite them out to lunch, invite them to gigs, give them freebies, be helpful to them.

Synergy

Encarta describes synergy as 'The interaction of two or more agents or forces so that their combined effect is greater than the sum of the individual effects.' Roughly translated – two heads are better than one – especially when both benefit from the alliance. In music industry terms anyone who will benefit from

Photo by Russell Persky

Tim Scott

Bassist, Singer, Songwriter

Act Rite Music (818) 705-0338

your success will have an interest in helping you to become successful, so synergy is an extremely useful concept on which to focus, whether it is with a manager, promoter, record company, publisher or a sponsor.

Tim Scott's site is at
http://www.timscott.com

Sponsorship

Most people imagine that before you can secure a sponsorship deal you will already need to be successful and established. For some companies that will undoubtably be true. Pepsi, as yet, have not show any signs of signing up any unknown acts to their fold, but not all companies have the same outlook. Many companies are constantly on the lookout for sponsorship opportunities. Whether they will be interested in sponsoring a band or artist will depend on the type of audience they want to reach. A clothing company, for example, which caters to the teenage to thirty-something sector of the population will be more likely to be interested in sponsoring an upcoming band or artist than would, say, a company which manufactures paint (although, with the promotion industry being as creative as it is you never can tell).

I'm Benny Rietveld

...sed in Hawaii. I spent many years touring and recording with **Miles Davis** and **Carlos Santana**, among others. I also write music for myself (some of wh... ...a music for Computer Gaming World, Sprint's Web site, etc...

That's right... a "content provider"...

ENTER

Benny Rietveld is at
www.bennyworld.com

As soon as you start filling the venues you are playing the time is right to investigate sponsorship opportunities. When you come across a company that you think will be targeting the type of people you have in your audience get in contact with them. Find out who deals with sponsorship in the company, send them your promotion package and invite them to one of your gigs.

Make sure the gig you invite them to is going to be well attended, and doesn't clash with an event which will rob you of a vast section of your audience (like a major sporting event, for example). Nothing will impress them less than an empty house.

Show your potential sponsor that you are worth the investment. Besides your ability to fill venues show them examples of the type of publicity you have received from the media, such as newspaper articles (see press releases). If you have been on TV or radio give them copies of those appearances too.

Be aware of what your sponsor is looking for. Their main requirements will be to get as much coverage as possible from their promotion budget, but they will be equally conscious of the need for whatever or whomever they sponsor to convey the right kind of image for their product or company.

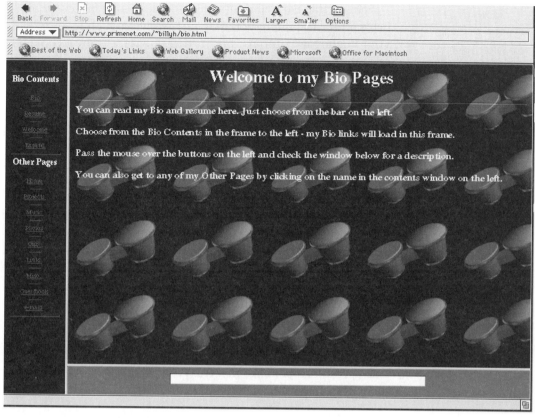

Billy Hulting's web page has pics, bio and music clips, and gig schedule. Take a look at www.zerobpm.com/billy/

Mailing list

Once you get around two thousand or so names on your mailing list that too will be a statistic to make sure a potential sponsor is aware of. Immediately it tells them that any advert or promotion they decide to make through your newsletter will automatically reach two thousand people who fit the profile of their target customers.

Treat your sponsor well

Once you secure a sponsorship deal it is tempting to take the money say 'Thank you very much,' and not give them another thought. Instead you should look at it as being just the beginning of a long term relationship. Give your sponsor progress reports. If they have advertised in your newsletter send them a copy of the newsletter, and if they have sponsored an event make sure they receive photographs of it – preferably photos which show their company logo on display. Not only will this highlight how good an investment you are, they might also choose to use details of your event in their own promotional literature so you'll gain publicity from their circulars too.

Sponsorship isn't all multi-million deals, sadly, but every bit helps. In the beginning you may just receive enough to keep your mailing list running, but further down the track it could be enough to finance a whole tour.

Creating a buzz

The key to all successful promotion lies in the ability to create interesting ways of attracting the public's attention. As the general public's needs become increasingly sophisticated, promotion teams are required to become more and more resourceful. If you are responsible for your own promotion it is easy to become buried by the volume of work it can entail. To avoid becoming burned out share the workload. Not only will it help to get the job done but you will also find it is easier keeping each other motivated than it is for one person to try to do so themselves.

Public relations consultants

PR people are the hired help of the music industry. Look in any of the music industry directories and you will find in their listings everyone from song pluggers and logo designers to fan club operators and image makers. Whatever your particular need there will be a professional to take care of it.

Your promotion package

Every band or artist needs to put together a promotion pack. What you decide to include in it will very much depend on the size of your budget. At the very least it should contain a biography, photos, demo tape (or preferably CD), performance reviews, and contact information. With a bigger budget you might consider adding a video tape, a sample of your merchandise or novelty items related to your current promotion. It is worthwhile giving some thought to the presentation of this material. The media receive promotion packages every day, so it will pay to make yours as appealing to them as possible.

Merchandising

Merchandising has always been a lucrative sideline for bands and artists but over the years has progressed far beyond the cheap 'T' shirts and records sold out of the back of the van. These days as more and more acts are becoming aware of the discriminating tastes of their fans they are going so far as to create their own designer lines of merchandise. Radiohead now promote their own brand of caps and sportswear and have launched their own merchandising outfit *Waste*.

Inevitably, one suspects, this will be just the beginning of a whole new trend within the music industry which will overshadow the more traditional selection of 'T' shirts, CDs, tapes, posters, tour books, badges and key-rings paraphanalia usually associated with touring merchandise.

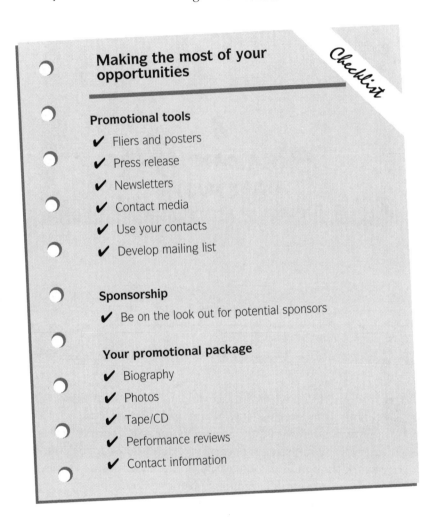

Making the most of your opportunities

Checklist

Promotional tools

- ✔ Fliers and posters
- ✔ Press release
- ✔ Newsletters
- ✔ Contact media
- ✔ Use your contacts
- ✔ Develop mailing list

Sponsorship

- ✔ Be on the look out for potential sponsors

Your promotional package

- ✔ Biography
- ✔ Photos
- ✔ Tape/CD
- ✔ Performance reviews
- ✔ Contact information

8
Taking care of the paperwork

* Keep copies of contracts
* Make every receipt count
* Advice from the tax man

* Frequently accepted tax deductions

A nything to do with contracts and accounts tends to be about as interesting as watching mud drying at an outdoor festival after everyone has gone home. – It's the bit that is left after all the fun stuff is over. If you don't take care of your paperwork though you could easily find yourself losing money needlessly or in a weak bargaining position should, as occasionally happens, during the tour you happen to be faced with a dispute over your contract, for example.

Keep copies of contracts and correspondence

Whether you are a band, solo artist or hired musician, it is always worth while taking copies of your contract (between you and your agent, venue or tour manager) on the road with you.

It is an unfortunately common occurrence for venues and agents to want to change parts of your agreement after you have turned up for your gig. Hotel venues in particular seem to be prone to this habit and often seem to think they will be able to ask you to play for longer hours (with or without extra pay) or that they can change your performance schedule. Instead of the three one hour sets you had agreed to you might discover on your arrival that they want you to play a half hour on half hour off arrangement. This would mean the same duration of play but over six hours instead of three. If you have a copy of your contract with you you will be in a stronger position when it comes to voicing any grievance rather than having to say 'I left my contract at home but I'm sure it said ...' Similarly they may have agreed to cover certain costs stated in your contract but at the time of paying you 'forget' to include these in your fee. Those kind of issues tend to be easier to rectify if you have a copy of the original contract at hand.

＊ TIP ＊

Warning: If you agree to change anything that is stated in your original agreement, technically this means that the contract has been broken. If just a small portion is being altered – say for example, you have agreed to play an extra set but for an additional payment – make sure you have this in writing, signed by all the parties who signed the original agreement, and include a clause which states something to the effect of 'All other terms and conditions remain as stated in the original agreement.'

Make every receipt count

As most musicians will be recognised (for tax purposes) as being self-employed, good receipt management is a process well worth cultivating. All too often receipts end up in hotel room wastepaper baskets when instead they could go home with you and be a justifiable expense to offset against your tax bill. Big or small they all help so it is worthwhile hanging onto them until you can hand them over to your accountant when you get back home.

Advice from the tax man

Each country has its own quirks and foibles when it comes to what you can or cannot claim as a legitimate expense on your Tax Return. To find out what these are for your country contact your local tax department and ask for a copy of their guidelines. If you have an accountant they too will be able to supply you with all the information you need.

Frequently accepted tax deductions

Tools of your trade

Any instrument or piece of equipment which you use for your work is usually an accepted deductible expense. If you buy more gear on the road keep copies of receipts along with a copy of any Import Duty you end up paying (if applicable.) Tools of the trade also covers items such as guitar straps, strings, drum sticks etc.

Repairs

If you have had any of the tools of your trade repaired you should be able to offset those invoices against your earnings. In some circumstances you may also be able to include the cost of hiring equipment while the damaged equipment was being repaired as part of your expenses.

Insurance

Equipment insurance and Public Liability Insurance are usually recognised as business expenses.

Stage clothes

Mostly, stage clothes are seen to be a legitimate expense but there can be exceptions. Some taxation departments only allow you to claim a clothing deduction if the clothes are only worn on stage. If your stage gear is jeans and T shirts which you wear off-stage as well they might not count.

Travel expenses

Any travelling expenses which you incur solely for the purposes of your work are normally justifiable deductions.

Hotel accommodation

As above, if your hotel bill is the result of your work, your hotel bill will normally be one you can offset against your tax (unless it is paid by someone else).

Telephone

It would be nice if you could claim all of your phone bills, but your tax department will probably restrict your tax concession to phone calls related to business only. As this is sometimes hard to differentiate from your personal calls, some tax offices allow you to claim a percentage of your entire bill as a business expense. Good news if they give you a high percentage and you have a serious phone habit.

Deductions the tax man is unlikely to accept

Your mini-bar bill

Bills for non-accidental damage (i.e. wrecked hotel rooms.)

Parking tickets

Taking care of the paperwork

Checklist

✔ Keep copies of your contract and correspondence with you

✔ Make sure that any changes to the original contract are confirmed in writing and signed by all parties

✔ Find out what expenses your Tax Advisor will accept as taxable deductions

✔ Keep all business chargeable receipts

9
Women on the road

> You might as well get used to being called a 'girl' because it's better than 'chick', and 'woman' doesn't feature in the rock 'n roll vocabulary.
>
> *Julie Homi (keyboards: Peter Cetera, Yanni, Robert Palmer)*
> *Keyboard Review Magazine.*

Although both male and female musicians share many of the same 'road' experiences there are times when the gender difference leaves them poles apart. Inevitably there will be instances when even the most vehement of non-feminists will find herself uttering the words 'This wouldn't be happening if I were male.' It could be something as innocuous as turning up for a gig and being told that you won't be allowed in to set up your gear until the male members of the band get there (presumably – because they don't think you know how to plug into a mains socket). Then again, there will be times when you will need to overcome the 'girlies can't play' prejudice which exists within some circles (because the X chromosome is not renowned for carrying musical talent, apparently); and then there may even be instances where you will experience full-blown sexual harassment. And that is just your working life. Off stage and travelling through culturally diverse territories can provide moments which are just as challenging. Knowing what to expect can go a long way towards making your touring experience a less frustrating one.

> ' Why is it that men who make their own decisions are strong, and women who do are control freaks? '
> *Sheryl Crow (on sexism within the music business) interview with Metro for The Times.*

The female musician's working life

Like it or not, as every female musician knows, the music industry is still one of male domination. In recent years it has come forward in leaps and bounds but still the female muso will, from time to time, find herself having to overcome outdated stereotypes before being accepted as anything more than the 'token babe' of the band or tour. The good news is that as more and more women enter the scene it is a situation which is always improving. Whether female and male musicians will ever be viewed in completely the same light remains to be seen though. Currently there are noticeable differences when it comes to accepted behaviour.

> ' As a woman in a largely male environment, sometimes you can really feel like the odd person out. Women are usually treated just like one of the guys in the band (no special treatment in other words), but are often not considered one of the guys enough to be included in their social plans and can end up feeling a bit left out. I learned how to compensate for that by just becoming super independent. I love to explore new cities and often just hit the pavement to see what's around me as soon as I hit a new town. I've had wonderful adventures all around the world because I took the initiative to go exploring on my own. If we were in a foreign country, I would often extend my stay past when the rest of the band

returned home and play super tourist for a week or so. **"**
Susie Davis (keyboards: Billy Idol, Sinead O'connor, Van Morrison).

Relationships on the road

Perhaps the most frequently occurring advice from women musicians is that which concerns the emotional side to life on the road. The pressures and the joys of the tour are apt to cause tour members to become more involved with each other than they would under normal circumstances. Although enjoyable at the time, an intimate relationship with a crew member may end up affecting the rest of your entourage in a surprising number of ways – some of which will not be positive.

' Avoid becoming romantically or sexually involved with anyone in the organization. This is much easier said than done. The road can be a lonely place, and most of us want to cuddle up with someone at the end of the night. However, it is far safer to make new friends along the way (or fly old ones in) than to complicate your professional life with personal entanglements. The recommendation to avoid sexual involvements with co-workers holds especially true for women. Often, a woman is in the minority on a tour, and jealousy and resentment can develop if she starts shacking up with one of the guys. I find it safer to think of myself as one of the guys, or maybe their sister. I don't mind doing a little mothering now and then, as long as they don't take it for granted. **"**
Julie Homi (keyboards: Peter Cetera, Yanni, Robert Palmer).

In some circumstances the female musician (or male – come to that) may find her or himself on the receiving end of unwanted attention from another crew member. Although this can be tedious, in many instances it can be resolved early and easily by making your disinterest clear right from the start. Keeping a sense of humour about the situation will help avoid causing a bad atmosphere.

' Women can sometimes experience special problems if they become viewed sexually by another member of the entourage, but in general I was always treated respectfully by the men I worked with and for. On one tour, our drummer refused to hang out with me because he said he was sexually frustrated and I made the problem worse, but anybody who's controlled

by their libido should be kept clear of anyway.**"**
Susie Davis (keyboards: Billy Idol, Sinead O'connor, Van Morrison).

If you have a problem which persists and you find it becoming increasingly hard to retain a sense of humour you should bring it to the attention of your tour manager and recruit his help to resolve the situation. For the most part though, market forces and the increasing demands for professionalism have made the modern tour evolve into a more workable and less hedonistic version of itself compared to a decade or so ago.

"Gigging today is very different. Buses are better equipped and safer. Gear in general works better and is better designed. Promoters are more scrutinized and don't screw the bands over as much. There's more concentration on the music than throwing TVs out of hotel windows, more of a disease scare so the wild sex orgies aren't as stupid and rampant, there's more competition so the music and sound systems are much better.**"**
Dawayne Bailey (guitar: Bob Seger, Chicago).

To give the impression that nothing wild and exciting happens on tour would paint a false picture, though. No member of the entourage can avoid being totally unaffected by the whole performing experience. As every musician knows, performing in front of a crowd is a huge ego boost and then to come off stage and find yourself surrounded by people who want to speak to you, or want your autograph, or have ambitions to seduce you, is an empowering experience. It is not always easy for individuals to use that sudden sense of empowerment in healthful and constructive ways. That type of headiness coupled with the fast paced nature of the tour tends to encourage reckless behaviour, some of which may require you to put effort into being open minded and non-judgemental when it concerns your fellow crew members.

"I recommend tolerance: let boys be boys. Many male musicians like going to strip clubs. Some guys may bring groupies around. Some may be cheating on their wives. It's an unstated code of the road that all this is kept within the group. As a woman, I have mixed feelings about these behaviors, but as a member of a tour, I understand it is important that we all feel comfortable, and are free to do what we want offstage.**"**
Julie Homi (keyboards: Peter Cetera, Yanni, Robert Palmer).

Advice clinic with Susie Davis

Q What advice would you give a female musician about life on the road?

A My advice is to just be cautious about entering into romantic liaisons with members of the touring entourage. Women in general can tend to imbue a sexual relationship with more emotional meaning than a man might, and if a man breaks things off or behaves in a disrespectful way it can be devastating, especially because the touring environment can be very lonely, even with all those people around. A tour should be a fun and adventurous time and your main responsibility is to stay healthy, play well and keep a good attitude. Remember that it's hard on everybody, and the more supportive you are of each other the better time everyone will have. I've seen too many women, upset over a road relationship gone sour, who let it ruin the overall experience for them. I'm just saying to be wary, because the wrong decision can change your overall perception of a tour, and you deserve to have as good a time as you possibly can. One woman I worked with had a romance with a musician from another band on the tour, got pregnant, got dumped, and then had to get an abortion and her resulting grief and depression over the whole thing affected everybody down to the bus drivers. So women, be wise...
Susie Davis (keyboards: Billy Idol, Sinead O'connor, Van Morrison).

Leaving the West behind

Q What's the difference between a female musician and a terrorist?

A You can reason with a terrorist

If you are a westerner touring in the western world you will experience appreciable differences while moving from country to country or state to state, but these will be minor compared to the contrast of touring the Middle East or Asia. Travelling that far afield you will experience such vast differences in terms of social behaviour and cultural protocol it will be all too easy to feel like an alien visiting another planet. And being a woman can add to that sense of alienation. The cultural adjustment is much easier to make when you have at least a general idea of what to expect.

The Middle East

A woman with strong feminist views is likely to find the Middle East difficult to come to terms with. From the western perspective a Muslim woman's lifestyle might seem outdated and old fashioned, but in the Middle East the role of mother and matriarch of the household is one of utmost importance. It is a traditional role which is taken very seriously by both the women and men alike and is one that Islam, as a religion, is invested in protecting. As a result women have a number of strict social codes they are expected to follow – some of which western women are advised to comply with also. Approaching your visit to the Middle East with an open mind will give you an insight into a fascinating culture. A closed mind is likely to make your experience problematic and considerably less enjoyable.

Attitudes to western women

Unfortunately, TV and western movies have given Middle Eastern men a corrupted perception of western women. Images of promiscuous women who go around provocatively dressed and who will jump into bed with any male, with little or no encouragement, have given them the impression that all western women behave in this way. When they see women 'brazenly' exposing themselves by wearing shorts or sleeveless or backless tops this only helps to enforce this misconception. It is not something they are accustomed to seeing in their own culture so therefore their interpretation is that there must be some truth behind this notion of 'looseness.' As a result a western woman is likely to experience a degree of harassment.

If you go out on your own be prepared to be stared at or to be on the receiving end of suggestive comments and propositions. You may even be followed and at times discover that given the opportunity (like, for example, when you are in the middle of a crowd) such interest may become physically intrusive.

Although undoubtedly a nuisance, most of your experiences will barely rise above the level of schoolboy smut though. Serious crimes against women such as physical violence and rape are virtually unheard of in the Middle East.

Dos and don'ts in the Middle East

Do dress conservatively. Muslim women dress to cover their whole body in loose fitting clothes which will not reveal their shape. Western women, likewise, should avoid figure hugging clothing and ensure that most of their body is covered. Jeans are okay, but in the less liberally minded countries such as Saudi Arabia, Kuwait and Iran you will need to wear something loose fitting over the top, such as a long lined blouse which reaches below your knees. Tops should be similarly loose fitting and with long sleeves.

Don't make eye contact with strange men. It is interpreted as an invitation.

Do take someone with you if you are sightseeing as having a companion makes you less of a target.

Don't respond to any personal comments or remarks, instead act as though you didn't hear them.

Don't sit in the front seat of taxis. This is a men–only seat.

Do wear a wedding ring (sometimes referred to as a 'wolf deterrent') even if you are single. A married woman is viewed with more respect than an unmarried one and doing so will help discourage unwelcome attention from local men.

Do sit in the family seating area of restaurants. This is the area designated for women and children. If you don't you probably will not be served anyway or will be asked to move.

Do wear a bra or you will not only find yourself the focus of unwelcomed attention but will also be the cause of major traffic accidents on the roads. This is not an overstatement. As any western woman who has visited the Middle East will confirm, merely stepping out onto the street is enough to instigate the squealing of tyres. It is common for drivers to be so distracted that they drive into the back of the car in front of them or kerb their car on the pavement. To do anything that would cause drivers to be even more distracted would be dangerous for everyone in the vicinity at the time.

Dos and don'ts checklist

Checklist

Dos

✔ Dress conservatively

✔ Wear shorts and T shirts and bathing costumes at the pool or beach but not around town

✔ Take someone with you when you go sightseeing

✔ Wear a wedding ring as a deterrent

✔ Sit in the area designated for families

✔ Wear a bra

Don'ts

✔ Wear figure hugging or flesh revealing clothes

✔ Wear shorts and T shirts out in public

✔ Make eye-contact with strange men

✔ Respond to lewd and suggestive remarks

✔ Sit in the front seat of taxis

Dress codes

Casual western wear such as shorts, T shirts, and bathing costumes are appropriate for beside the hotel pool or in an accommodation compound, but not elsewhere.

Headwear and when to wear it

Headwear can be a needlessly worrisome issue. Western woman are usually not required to cover their hair except in the more strict states of Saudi Arabia, Kuwait and Iran, when they are expected to make sure all parts of their body are covered except for hands, feet and face, and their hair should be covered by a head-scarf (a hat is not appropriate – it needs to be a head-scarf).

What to take with you

Feminine hygiene

Besides anything you need to take which is work related there are some important items which can be hard to find in the Middle East. Tampons are not always readily available and even when they are you will not have the selection of brand names to choose from that you are used to. It is worthwhile taking your own supply with you.

Condoms

Surprisingly, condoms can be found fairly easily in the large supermarkets. There are however, a couple of good reasons for you to take your own supply. Firstly, they are not always as good a quality or reliability as the name brands you are likely to be more familiar with, and secondly, given the Middle Eastern suspicions of Western women it could invite trouble to be seen buying them.

Safety

In general a woman will be safer in the Middle East than she would be in any western country. Reported crimes against women are virtually unheard of in the region, but it would be foolish to be lulled into complacency as a result of low statistics. Exercise caution at all times and avoid taking risks when it comes to your own personal safety.

Taxis

Taking taxis rides is part of the cultural experience for every traveller. For western women in the Middle East most taxi journeys involve a sequence of questions which induces a sense of *deja vu* with each taxi ride. The first question will be 'how old are you?' You can answer that one as truthfully or not as you choose. The second question will be 'are you married?' Advice on how you answer that one depends on how long your journey is going to be. If you say 'no,' you are going to spend the rest of the journey being asked to provide detailed information explaining why. If you say 'yes' (another good reason for wearing the 'wolf deterrent' wedding band) the next one will be 'do you have children?' Say 'no,' to this one and you will be offered everything from sympathy to queries about your husband's ability to procreate followed by the offer of an introduction to meet 'my brother, he has many children. You meet him – I'm sure he can help.' Rapidly the single female traveller becomes adept at conjuring up a husband, family and whole family history to satisfy taxi drivers' conversational demands. But also be prepared to supply photographic evidence as authentication.

The Far East

Asia is much more female friendly and less antagonistic to feminist philosophies but although less restrictive in comparison to the Middle East women still have a clearly defined role in Eastern culture.

It is unusual for women to be in their late twenties and still single. This might be partly responsible for the Far Eastern fascination with age. Don't be surprised if the first question someone asks you is 'how old are you?' It will be common to find yourself on the receiving end of other equally direct questions. A westerner would think it rude to be so personal but it is a matter of course in Asia and no rudeness is intended.

What to take with you

Similar to the Middle East there will be some items which although readily available in the west will be harder to come by in the East.

Feminine hygiene

Take your own supply of tampons with you. Surprisingly, deodorants can be hard to find as well, so take what you will need with you.

Advice clinic with Carol Kaye

Q What advice would you give a female musician about life on the road?

A Be sure to have your own room and don't fall in love with anybody in the band, keep your distance, but enjoy the musicians like brothers. *Carol Kaye (bass: Hampton Hawes)*.

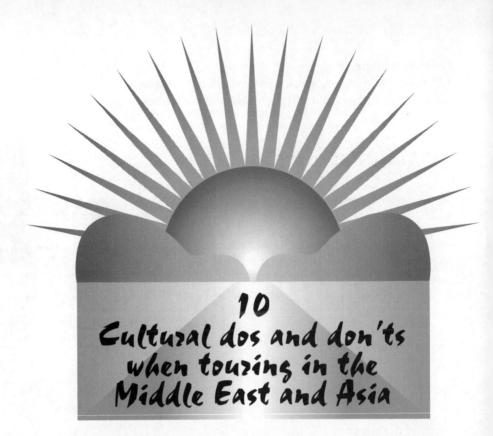

10
Cultural dos and don'ts when touring in the Middle East and Asia

The Middle East

* Alcohol
* Calls to prayer
* Religious songs
* Explicit songs
* Ramadan
* Stage wear
* Dress code
* Photographing

* Sex and taboos
* Theft
* Sexual harassment
* Western women in the Middle East
* Segregation
* Hands and feet

The Far East

* Bowing
* Handshaking
* Drinking
* Be mindful of space
* Shoes
* Business cards

* Visiting
* The gross out
* Taxis
* Climbing the language barrier
* Learning to live like an alien

This chapter could also be called 'the things you need to know to prevent yourself from being deported'.

As most musicians testify one of the best parts about being on the road is not only having the opportunity to visit foreign countries and experience different cultures, but that you actually get paid to do so. Touring musicians are fortunate enough to see parts of the world that most people only can when they are on vacation, plus they have the added bonus of someone else picking up the tab for all their travel, food, and accommodation costs, too.

‘ Seeing the world on someone else's budget. ’
Kevin Dukes (guitar: Boz Scaggs, Don Henley, Jackson Browne) on the best part about touring.

It would, though, be unwise to think of life on the road as being nothing more than a paid holiday with a bit of performing on the side. The touring schedule exposes the musician to much more than a demanding workload. Whereas most people are only on vacation for a couple of weeks at a time, musicians are on the road for longer periods and, travelling from country to country, frequently find that each stop on their itinerary brings a whole new set of rules in terms of protocol and accepted behaviour. This is particularly noticeable for westerners touring the Middle East and Far East. Conduct which is perfectly acceptable in the west can be interpreted as being offensive to other cultures. Often a cultural blunder might present nothing more than embarrassment for the person who makes it but in some instances it could mean a night in a prison cell, or even deportation.

Q & A with Benny Rietveld

Q What are the good bits about touring?

A Going to places you would normally never go to. Lots of time to think about things.

Q What are the bad bits?

A Going to places you would normally never go to. Lots of time to think about things.
Benny Rietveld (bass: Santana, Sheila E, Miles Davis).

The Middle East

The Middle East's tolerance of the western lifestyle varies markedly from territory to territory. The United Arab Emirates (of which Dubai and Abu Dhabi are a part) is a more liberally minded region than Saudi Arabia, Iran or Kuwait. The punishment for breaking the rules in the latter countries will tend to be more severe than a westerner would expect in their own country.

Alcohol

Parts of the Middle East are recognised as being 'dry' states, 'dry' meaning no alcohol – which is an alarming thought for many musicians. Each dry state has rules and regulations unique to their region, and in some cases this will mean that although officially a dry state, alcohol could still be available in the bar of your hotel. If it is, this facility will be for the exclusive use of hotel guests or private club members only.

In some dry states, musicians who are on extended contracts and are classed as resident expatriates will be able to apply for a liquor license. The license allows the holder to buy a restricted amount of alcohol each month (except during Ramadan when alcohol purchase is forbidden) for their own household's consumption only. Non-dry states (such as the UAE) have pubs and bars available to all expatriates.

* TIP *

Warning: In a dry state it is illegal to give away or sell alcohol. Punishment is quite severe and offenders can find themselves sentenced to lashes plus a spell in prison (anything up to several months) followed by deportation.

Calls to prayer

The Middle East, as a region, is officially Islamic. Followers of Islam are called to prayer five times a day, and these prayer sessions are broadcast by loudspeakers from mosques throughout each city, and in some areas, simultaneously on TV and radio too. Although westerners are not expected to attend the call to prayer (and in many regions they will be barred from doing so unless they are Muslim), they are expected to respect the prayer sessions by not interrupting or competing with them. If you are scheduled to be performing outdoors during the day or evening check that your performance time doesn't clash with one of the calls to prayer. If it does and you can't rearrange the schedule you may have to pause for the four minutes of prayer time. The organiser will be able to advise you on the correct protocol. The calls to prayer change by a minute or so each day. Prayer times are posted in daily newspapers.

Religious songs

Some Islamic states are highly sensitive about non-Islamic religions and will not tolerate Christian or other religious songs. It is a restriction which not even fame can always transcend. Sister Sledge during their tour of the Gulf in 1992 found that in Qatar they were requested not to sing 'Brother to Brother' because of its Christian message.

Explicit songs

Censorship is strict so avoid performing songs which have overtly sexual lyrics or which feature graphic language. Songs which even feature the word 'sex' will not be played on radio or TV. Live performances tend to have a greater degree of freedom though, largely because the lyrics are not so easy to distinguish.

Ramadan

The holy month of Ramadan falls on the ninth month of the lunar year. Traditionally, Ramadan is a month of abstention when Muslims are expected to focus on the teachings of the Koran and on spiritually purifying themselves by refraining from eating, drinking, smoking and sexual intercourse between the hours of sunrise and sunset. The fasting requirement means that many shops, businesses and restaurants will close during the day (or operate on restricted hours) and stay open late at night. Westerners are expected to respect the fast by not consuming any food or drink (not even water) in public, between the hours of sunrise and sunset. Live entertainment, and the selling of alcohol is not permitted during the holy month, so resident musicians will find that their contracts finish at the beginning of Ramadan or that they will not start until after Ramadan.

Ramadan begins
31 December 1998
20 December 1999
9 December 2000
28 November 2001
17 November 2002

Like the calls to prayer, Ramadan is constantly on the move and does not fall on the same date each year. Each successive Ramadan falls approximately eleven days before the date of the previous year's.

❛Getting the opportunity to visit other countries and experience their cultures is probably the greatest benefit of getting to tour. I've had some wonderful adventures in many countries of the world, and I was being paid the whole time.❜
Susie Davis (keyboards: Billy Idol, Go West, Debbie Harry).

Stage wear

Bearing in mind the region's conservatism regarding clothing, both male and female musicians need to exercise some caution regarding their stage wear. Female musicians need to be aware that their stage clothes during tours of the Middle East ought to be fairly conservative and should not be too revealing or figure hugging. Men too should not wear tightly fitting clothing or expose a bare chest.

The less liberally minded regions usually have a government official attending the performance to make sure that no boundaries of taste or decency are breached. If an outfit is thought to be too lewd or alluring they may stop the show or refuse to grant the venue permission to stage any future performances. It is reported that when Tina Turner performed in Doha (years before her re-emergence as a superstar) her outfit was so stunning that it was another two years before any venue in the state was allowed to stage a popular music concert again.

Dress code

The protocol regarding clothing varies enormously throughout the Middle Eastern region. In general, to avoid offence, both men and women should be conservative with their dress outside of the hotel or apartment compound. Swimming and beach wear is fine by the pool but is rarely acceptable elsewhere. Aim to cover as much flesh as possible. For men this means wearing trousers instead of shorts and for women, long sleeved tops and either trousers or long skirts. Even though failure to do so affects women more than men (when they could find themselves having to fend off unwelcomed attention from some of the local men, or even being spat at) men also will find themselves the subject of ridicule if they get the dress code wrong.

' For me, I still enjoy travelling. I know people that get burned out on it but I just like seeing other places – I like going to other towns. With your schedule though you're usually just in and out so if you want to see a town you've got to have a plan about how much time you've got and what you want to see. Take cabs and go to places of interest. '
Tim J. Scott (bass: Tower of Power, Stevie Wonder).

Photographing

If you are out and about sight-seeing with a camera or video camera you need to be aware that, although Arabic women covered from head to foot in black might seem like an interesting shot to take home and show friends and family, your subject will not tolerate you attempting to do so. You will also receive a hostile reaction if you are seen photographing the royal palaces, or anything which is viewed by the host nation as having military importance. This will include airports and train stations, but the military connection is not always obvious so photographers are advised to exercise caution. If you are caught you can expect to have your camera film and/or your photographic equipment confiscated.

Sex and taboos

One of the hardest facets of Islamic society for westerners to grasp is the Muslim beliefs regarding relationships. Marriages are arranged and therefore dating is not a recognised part of their culture. Sex outside of marriage is completely taboo and in the less liberal states any couples caught engaging in sexual activity (or suspected to be) could face imprisonment – whether they are Muslim or not.

Prostitution

Nowhere near as common place as it is in the western world but occasionally prostitution does hit the newspaper headlines, usually attached to a story which reports that a number of foreign women have been rounded up, punished and deported. Officially prostitution is not tolerated – for the same reasons as above.

Theft

The Middle East has crime statistics that put the the western world to shame. Incidences of theft and violent crime are minimal compared to the west. Whether this is due to the severity of the punishment for offenders or an ingrained part of the culture is not easy to determine, but – kleptomaniac musicians beware – the bottom line is that crime is not viewed at all leniently, whether malicious or just mischievous. What may seem to some as nothing more than a prank may not be viewed in the same light by a non-westerner.

' We'd had a few beers and when we came out of the hotel saw a bus next to the taxi rank. The engine was running but no one was in it so we thought we'd take it for a spin – just for the hell of it. Twenty minutes later the police pulled us over. We had our passports confiscated and spent a week in jail ' *(name withheld by request).*

Sexual harassment

Men

Even though sexual harassment is most often associated with women it is by no means exclusively their domain. In the Middle East men too should be prepared to encounter interest from male admirers. It is not uncommon for western men to be propositioned while visiting a restaurant or walking out on the streets. Slightly confusingly though there may be moments when a man will think he is being propositioned when, in fact, he is only experiencing Arabic courtesy. It is a common gesture in the region for men to take hold of another's hand or arm when they are directing them somewhere or assisting them. The gesture does not have the connotation that the western world has attached to it.

Women

As described in the previous chapter, western women travelling through the Middle East can expect to experience a degree of sexual harassment. The popular myth that all western women are sexually 'available' means that, sooner or later, during your travels you will find yourself being stared at or on the receiving end of rude or suggestive remarks as you pass by. In general these rarely raise beyond the Arabic equivalent of construction workers' catcalls, but if you encounter more persistent attention, or find yourself being followed, stay calm and avoid confrontation. Instead, where possible, head for a more populated area, or failing that, go to the nearest hotel lobby or shopping area.

Taxis

Taxis are metered. To avoid argument when you reach your destination make sure that the meter is turned on as soon as you start your journey. Some drivers will attempt to persuade you to agree to a set fare instead of using the meter (which will be more expensive, naturally), but if you insist on a metered fare they will usually comply.

   Women should not sit in the front seat as this is for men only (for more on women and taxis see previous chapter).

Western women in the Middle East

Unmarried female musicians under the age of 35 may sometimes experience difficulties in getting their visas approved in a non UAE state. In some areas it will be virtually impossible. Saudi Arabia largely excludes single women who are employed in any other profession besides medicine or teaching. Married women will be more readily accepted, especially if they are accompanied by their husbands (see also the previous chapter).

Segregation

Some cafes, restaurants, juice bars etc. have different seating areas for men and women. Quite often the women's section will be referred to as the family seating area.

Hands and feet

Many cultures have issues about footwear. In the Middle East it is considered offensive to show the soles of your feet. So, if you are sitting with your legs crossed, make sure the soles of your shoes are facing the floor and are not directed at anybody.

In the Arabic world the left hand is considered to be unclean because it is associated with toilet purposes. If you are giving or receiving something you should do so with your right hand. Likewise, when eating you should use your right hand.

Middle East dos and don'ts

Checklist

Dos

✔ Dress conservatively

✔ Respect the call to prayer sessions

✔ Exercise caution when sightseeing with your camera

Don'ts

✔ Sell or give alcohol away in a dry state

✔ Play loud music during the calls to prayer

✔ Perform religious songs

✔ Perform sexually explicit songs or songs with obscene lyrics

✔ Photograph Arabic women or anything which could have military significance

✔ Direct the soles of your shoes at anyone

✔ Give or receive anything with your left hand

Q & A With Julie Homi

Q What are the good bits of touring?

A Enthusiastic audiences, getting paid to travel to exotic places, seeing old friends, being treated like a celebrity, road romances, days off, watching videos in the back lounge of the bus, meeting celebrities, knowing I did a great show that night.
Julie Homi (Keyboards: Peter Cetera, Yanni, Robert Palmer).

Far East

Not only is the Far East one of the most fascinating regions of the world to visit, it also happens to be a veritable minefield when it comes to opportunities for cultural misunderstandings. Just as the West and East are on opposite sides of the planet, so too can they seem to be equally polarised when it comes to accepted behaviour. As a result, westerners often appear to be gifted when it comes to making blunders or unintentional insults. The good news is that such blunders are usually accepted as such and are not likely to result in the sort of severe punishment administered in regions like the Middle East. However, what makes cultural etiquette within the Far East even more confusing for westerners is that the rules are different for each region.

Bowing

It is an area in which many westerners feel uncomfortable and inhibited but bowing is a vital part of Eastern manners, so learn to bow when bowed to or when greeting someone. On the surface it sounds like it should be a simple procedure but foreigners commonly make a few mistakes. First, they decide that a nod is acceptable as a bow, which sometimes it is, but if you nod in response to a deep bow this will appear to be rude as it implies that you think you are of a much higher status than the person who bowed. Also, avoid bowing too quickly as a frantic bob tends to look hysterical and your hosts will find it so too.

Handshaking

Don't offer your hand unless someone offers his first. Physical contact in general is understated. Hugging is not a widely accepted part of Far Eastern culture, and even something as seemingly innocuous to a westerner as patting someone on the back will probably not be received appreciatively.

Drinking
Don't pour you own drinks. The accepted protocol is that you pour drinks for others and then wait for someone to pour yours.

Be mindful of space
Use a small amount of space when travelling on trains, buses, planes, etc. Foreigners have a habit of behaving just as they would in their own country and tend to spread their luggage out over the seats and sprawl with legs crossed or arms stretched out. This is not possible to do in a region as densely populated as Asia. Stow your luggage in the areas provided and be prepared to share your space with more people than you would have imagined possible.

Shoes
Shoes are considered dirty in the Far East so never put your feet up on the furniture or on a bus or train seat. If you do you will find yourself reprimanded. Even small children are taught to take their shoes off before they crawl around on furniture.

Be prepared to take your shoes off at the doors of all houses and apartments as well as many public places. Some people worry about when or where they should remove their shoes but it isn't a big deal if you follow the cues. Whenever you come across shoes in an entrance way it's a safe bet that yours should join them. If there is a set of slippers outside the bathroom these should be used to avoid 'contaminating' your house slippers while you are using the bathroom. These are not to be worn around the house and should be removed as soon as you leave the bathroom.

Business cards
Business cards should be presented and received using both hands. When receiving a card you should study it carefully, as a mark of respect, and not just glance at it and shove it inside your wallet or pocket.

Visiting

If you visit someone's home you should take a gift. Something from your own country, or something you can eat or drink will make a good choice. But avoid giving anything which would be seen to be obviously cheap or tacky.

The gross out

Westerners will often be appalled at the amount of spitting that goes on in some Asian countries, but by the same token there are times when westerners' behaviour can seem equally unrefined. Nose blowing is one of the western habits which has no home in Eastern society. To actually blow your nose into a kleenex and then put it in your pocket is the double whammy of gross behaviour, but just as westerners will be able to offend non-westerners, so too will you find that, at times, non-westerners can manage to unintentionally offend the western world's sense of political correctness. It helps if all these instances can be viewed with an equal amount of equanimity.

Q & A with Gene Williams

Q What's the worst/funniest/most memorable thing that has happened to you on the road?

A Hmmm ... would have to be the time in Japan when a local band asked me to stay to see their performance ... and after waiting in the club two hours for the set to start, they came on wearing black faces and Afro wigs. They didn't do it as an insult but I was so mad I left the club after their first song. A week later they saw me and asked me what I thought of their gig. I told them I respected them as musicians, but in the US wearing black face is an insult to African Americans. I wasn't sure if they understood due to the obvious language barrier, but a week later I was again invited to their next show, and was happy to see they no longer wore the black face make up.
Gene Williams (keyboards: Tours: Roberta Flack, Chaka Khan, Joe).

Taxis

As with anywhere else in the world, make sure the taxi driver turns on the meter when you start your journey. This will avoid any argument about what your fare should be when you reach your destination.

In some parts of Asia (Korea is one region, for example) don't be surprised if your taxi driver takes other passengers on board besides yourself. It may be disconcerting at first to suddenly find yourself sharing a cab with several strangers but is an efficient way of dealing with the demand for their services – especially when it is raining and the demand for taxis far outweighs the number of taxis available. When you reach your destination you will normally be expected to pay the meter reading irrespective of how many shared the ride.

Travelling alone at night this practice can make anyone feel vulnerable, and if you are unfamiliar with the geography of the area you should make it clear to your driver that you do not wish to share. The driver may respond to your request with exasperation but as some regions (like Korea) have had well publicised problems in the past where lone foreigners have experienced mistreatment from taxi drivers (who after they have picked up a foreigner have stopped to pick up an accomplice to help them rob their passenger), such caution is understandable.

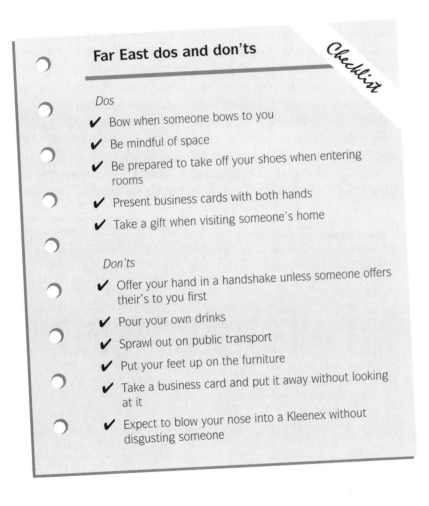

Far East dos and don'ts

Checklist

Dos

✔ Bow when someone bows to you

✔ Be mindful of space

✔ Be prepared to take off your shoes when entering rooms

✔ Present business cards with both hands

✔ Take a gift when visiting someone's home

Don'ts

✔ Offer your hand in a handshake unless someone offers their's to you first

✔ Pour your own drinks

✔ Sprawl out on public transport

✔ Put your feet up on the furniture

✔ Take a business card and put it away without looking at it

✔ Expect to blow your nose into a Kleenex without disgusting someone

Q & A with Dawayne Bailey

Q Have you ever experienced any memorable cultural problems touring overseas?

A The main cultural problem is just making sure you don't offend too many people in distinctively different places like Thailand, or really anywhere for that matter, with dumb behaviour or just being a 'rude American' – I've never experienced any problems personally, but I've seen people get over zealous and offend the natives.

Dawayne Bailey (guitar: Bob Seger, Chicago).

Climbing the language barrier

Although climbing the language barrier can at times seem like an Olympian feat there are an equal number of times when translations are memorable for their entertainment value.

In the past Korean taxi drivers have had a reputation for being discourteous to their passengers. In an effort to clamp down on hostile behaviour the government issued complaints cards displayed in the rear of taxis and listing a telephone number which passengers were invited to contact if they had any complaints. The service the telephone number connected them to was the 'Intercourse Discomfort Report Centre.'

Then, of course, there are the times when you come across translations which seem to have been made via Swahili.

Guest welcome note

August 28,

Dear Guest,

Everyday, from January 1st to today, frankly without missing a single day, I had a moment of prayer for your staying with us cozy, fluffy, comfortable like you are in your Lord's bosom, your staying at the (hotel's name withheld) safe, delightful, bright and clean like a place where the Lord stays, and your successful accomplishment of your wish in the best favourable sense. I hope my pray reaches to move the Lord works out well.

Thank you so much and wish you a thanking your Lord.

Sincerely,

Executive Assistant Manager

❝ One of the worst things that happened was when I was with Paul McCartney in Japan in 1980 and he got busted for pot, and the tour got washed out and we never got to do the tour. That was a shame 'cause I really wanted to tour Japan. I've only been to Japan once since then and that was to the Mount Fuji Jazz Festival, so although that was very nice I didn't really get to see the country, meet a lot of the people and the different places, and just see it extensively as I would have going to ten or fifteen cities like we were going to on that tour. So I guess that was about the worst thing that happened although it didn't really happen to me directly, it was just a bad situation. I've had minor things like vehicles break down and stuff like that, but never had anything really bad happen to me on the road. ❞

Steve Howard: horns (Paul McCartney, Ray Charles, Albert Collins) on the worse thing that's happened on tour.

Learning to live like an alien

You don't have to travel overseas or be in a country which doesn't speak your language to feel like an alien. Sometimes countries which claim to share the same common language can be just as confusing – as any American who has visited Europe, or European who has visited America, will confirm. Sometimes word usage or strong regional dialects can be be as discombobu-lating as etiquette. It is noticeable that Americans tend to have a harder time understanding Europeans than the other way around. Quite possibly this might be because Europeans have had the chance to 'learn' the subtle differences by watching American television programmes but for both such communication difficulties can be a frustrating experience.

Learning to live like an alien is the key to successful worldwide travelling.

❝ Seeing all kinds of people, all the tourist things, the fun of traveling can be good if the airlines are good, the connections are good the accommodations are good, eating out is fun if you find lots of good places. ❞

Carol Kaye (bass: Hampton Hawes) on the best things about touring.

11
Visas and passports

* You and your passport
* Applying for visas
* Your passport info
* What treatment to expect from an immigration officer
* Know your rights

Music, is not renowned for being one of the most stable professions in the universe. One moment your diary will have more empty spaces than gigs, and the next, you'll be packing to join a world tour. Everything can turn on a phone call. To be able to capitalise on such swings of fortune a musician needs to be prepared.

You and your passport

If you don't already have a passport, apply for one immediately. The application process can take six to eight weeks, and sometimes longer if you happen to be applying during peak holiday times. The chances are you will not get that much notice if you are being invited to join a tour or you or your band are replacing another act at the last minute.

If you already have a passport check its expiry date. If it is within nine months of needing to be renewed, apply for a new one. Some countries require passports to be valid for at least another six months from the day you arrive, even if you are only going to be there for a couple of weeks.

Which passport?

Europeans used to be able to apply for a one year or five year passport for travelling within the European community but these have been discontinued. Now everybody needs to have the full ten year passport.

Some travellers mistakenly think that if they are members of the European community visiting other countries which are also members, they will be able to travel without a passport. It is a myth. Every traveller needs a passport.

What do I need to apply for a passport?

You will need a passport application form (available from your local post office or passport issuing department), passport sized photographs, and your birth certificate. Non-nationals will need to include evidence of their legal right to apply for a passport, such as, proof of their legal right to residence, marriage certificate, etc.

What do I do if I have to get a passport in a hurry?

Getting a passport at short notice is a headache. Your best bet will be to first phone the passport issuing office and explain your situation. If they do not have a major backlog of passport applications and are sympathetic to your predicament they may be able to speed up the processing time and all you will have to do is send them all of the necessary application information and photographs etc. by express mail. If not you will have to go to the passport issuing office in person and wait around for what can be hours while they process the necessary information.

What should I do if I lose my passport?

At the very least a lost passport will mean a bad day, or if it is lost or stolen when you are travelling, several bad days. How quickly the situation will be resolved will depend on the issuing office or embassy you have to deal with. Some administrations will refuse to issue another passport until exhaustive enquiries have been made regarding how it came to be lost or stolen. While

☀ TIP ☀

Avoid getting aggressive with embassy or consulate staff. As frustrating as your predicament may be, it will be counter productive if you vent your frustrations on them. Remember, it is they who will determine how quickly you will be issued with new documentation.

☀ TIP ☀

Keep a couple of sets of photocopies of your passport on file so that they are ready to fax out as soon as the tour manager, venue, or promoter wants them. Also, make sure you have a couple of dozen passport sized photographs available, too. If you expect to be travelling a lot have a professional photographer take a 'decent' photograph of you (if there is such a thing as a decent passport photo), and get a copy of the negative so that you can have more printed later if you need them. It is much cheaper to do it that way and more convenient than having to find an instant photo booth at short notice and making do with what will usually be inferior quality pictures.

this is going on you will be unable to leave the country. If you are on tour not only will this mean you will be left behind but in most cases you will also not be paid for any gigs you miss as a result. On top of that you will have to pay for all your accommodation and food expenses you incur while you are separated from the rest of the tour.

In general, due to the lucrative black market trade of stolen passports worldwide, missing passports are treated with suspicion by government departments.

'The singer lost his passport with such frequency that the authorities began to make enquiries as to whether he might be selling them.'
Tom Doyle on Richard Ashcroft of The Verve (Q Magazine).

If you lose your passport abroad report to the nearest police department where you will be asked to file a statement on how it came to be lost, and then told to contact your local embassy or consulate. Later, you will need to visit them and supply them with copies of the police report.

On our way to Jakarta, Indonesia, my passport was lost/stolen on the plane. I say lost/stolen because I had left it on the plane when we stopped in Singapore to make a change and by the time I was allowed back on to look for it it had been taken. I couldn't get on the connecting flight so I was forced to wait in the airport until it could be located. Well – no such luck. I had to spend the night in the Singapore airport. Morning – still no word. I still had until that evening to get to the first show in Jakarta. Well – The US embassy was closed for a holiday so I was going to miss the show that night. I did, however, get Singapore immigration to release me into the city, unchaperoned, overnight with absolutely no identification. Cool, huh? I did get a new passport and work visa (imagine me not having changed clothes in two days, with long hair and earrings walking into the consulate of a Muslim country asking for a replacement for a work visa for which I didn't have the complete paperwork) and arrived at the venue in Jakarta 20 minutes before the first set. It seems almost funny now but it certainly wasn't then nor for many months to follow. I tell you – since then I have been in some tough and weird situations but they just don't bother me anymore.
Billy Hulting (percussion: Lou Rawls, Natalie Cole, Barry Manilow, Maynard Ferguson).

Applying for visas

If you are part of a touring group and are going to be performing overseas, in most circumstances you will need a visa (members of the European community do not need visas when visiting other countries within the community). Either your tour manager, the venue, or promoter will be responsible for getting the visa paperwork together but to do so they will need you to supply them with your passport information and, depending on the regions you will be touring, half a dozen or so passport sized photographs of yourself.

Your passport info

Whoever applies for your visa will need a photocopy of your passport. Some will just ask for a copy of the page which features your photograph and the passport details, but occasionally you will be asked for a photocopy of every page). In addition they will need to know:

Your passport number
Place it was issued
Date it was issued
When it expires

When photocopies are not enough
In most cases photocopies of your passport are enough to allow visa processing. The details are filed by the relevant embassies and the documentation is completed as you enter the country. In some instances, though, you will be asked to either hand over or send your passport to the nearest embassy of the country you will be visiting, for processing before your departure.

Lost paperwork
It happens, so whenever possible keep photocopies of irreplaceable documents just in case they go astray. Having a copy should make it possible to speed up the process when you are seeking replacement documents.

How long will it take to get a visa?
It depends on the country you are visiting and the nature of your visit. Musicians just passing through as part of a tour will usually find it quicker to get their visa processed than one whose contract is considered long term, (i.e. more than a month). Some visas will be granted on the spot (assuming you have presented

✳ TIP ✳
Don't take unnecessary risks with vital documentation. Even if you have never lost a piece of mail before, you can guarantee that as soon as you send your passport by regular mail that will be the last you will see of it. If you have to send your passport only do so by the safest registered or recorded delivery service available to you, and either collect it in person or make arrangements for it to be returned to you in the same way.

all the necessary and completed paperwork with the application), while others can take anything up to six weeks.

What do I do if I am not in my home country when I have to apply for a visa in another country?

This is a situation which effects long term, residential contract musicians more than the touring musician. If your residency abroad lasts for a month and you are wanting to process a visa for another country to start an engagement immediately after, it can be a problem – especially if the embassy of the country you are due to be travelling onwards to requests you to forward your passport to them, and if obtaining the visa is going to take some time.

If business travellers fulfill certain criteria they will be permitted to legally hold two passports. To be granted a second passport your need has to fall into one of two categories:

1 If you can prove that your business or career is being seriously compromised by the delays caused by visa application you have a case for applying for an additional passport. This is most useful for musicians who are hired on long term (a month or more) contracts, as in the above example, who are unable to part with their passport long enough for a visa application to be processed. The loss of work caused by this logistical problem is considered just cause for applying for an additional passport.
2 If your passport contains a stamp which will bar you from being allowed to enter another country (e.g. travellers who have visited Israel and have had their visit stamped in their passport are banned from entry into Arabic countries) some embassies will issue a second passport to overcome this handicap.

How do I apply for a second passport?

Write to your nearest embassy and explain your reasons for requiring an additional passport. Do not be surprised if their first response is one of reluctance though, as understandably, embassies are unwilling to issue a second passport unless they are absolutely convinced that it is necessary and that the additional documentation is going to be used correctly and legally. Persistence is the key. Once the embassy can see how detrimental holding a single passport can be for the 'residential' touring musician they will agree to your holding a second passport.

The blessing and the curse of the second passport

Holding two passports makes it possible to avoid losing contracts owing to visa application delays, but it can present you with a whopping problem if any immigration officer becomes aware you are carrying two of them. From an immigration officer's point of view, anyone seen to be travelling with two passports has either illegal or immoral intentions and they will challenge you accordingly. To avoid ugly interrogations be covert about the additional passport.

What treatment to expect from an immigration officer

Encountering Immigration and customs officials is probably the single most disconcerting part of travelling. At no other time are you likely to be in the position where one person is capable of seriously affecting the quality of your day. Unfortunately, to be able to predict what kind of treatment you will receive you need to be psychic. Suffice to say it will be somewhere between welcoming and downright inhospitable. Some territories are renowned for the hostility displayed by their Immigration officers. The USA has a reputation for being particularly officious with their foreign visitors, but you are just as likely to receive similar treatment anywhere in the world. Your own experience will have as much to do with how you respond to the immigration officer's questions, and the kind of day the officer is having more than current government legislation regarding foreign visitors.

How to avoid trouble

Musician travellers can avoid unnecessary trouble by making sure they are carrying all the required paperwork and documentation at the time of travelling. When entering a country you will be required to show that you have a valid passport, a visa (where necessary), an onward going air (or other transport) ticket which proves your intention to leave the country at a later date, and in some cases will want to see details of your employment contract. As long as your documentation is in order an immigration officer will have little reason to detain you for further questioning.

What is the difference between a visa and a work permit?

A visa grants a traveller permission to enter a country as a visitor but does not necessarily allow you to work in that

TIP

Immigration officers are extremely suspicious of anyone holding two passports. If they become aware of the extra passport they may consider it necessary to question you further (which could involve delaying you for several hours from continuing with the rest of your journey). It pays to be discreet about your additional passport.

TIP
Immigration officers have a reputation for being aggressive, suspicious and hostile even on their good days. It is tempting to respond in a similar manner but it pays you to avoid doing so. Even if their is nothing wrong with your paperwork, returned hostility may be enough to encourage them to hold you up or decide to search your baggage or you yourself more thoroughly.

country (although in some cases your visa will be a combined visa and work permit). A work permit enables the holder to be employed for the duration stated in the permit.

What happens if I work in a country but don't have a work permit?

If you are caught doing so you will probably be deported from that country and barred from entering it again for a set period which will usually run to several years.

I want to go to a country to check out the work opportunities over there. Can I do that?

Yes, but depending on your country of choice you will need to take extra care regarding your visa status and will need to bear in mind that part of the reason why immigration departments exist is to protect their home job market and actively dissuade foreigners from taking jobs in their country. Unless you have a job to go to you will not be entitled to apply for a work visa and will have to enter the country on a tourist visa. If you arrive as a tourist and are seen to be carrying promotional material such as photos, demo tapes and resumes the immigration officer will assume you are intending to look for work and therefore are intending to breach your tourist visa status, for which they will deny you entry. It sounds like petty bureaucracy, and bureaucracy is certainly what it is, but once you are aware of potential pitfalls it is easy to find a solution. In this example all you will need to do is make sure you mail your promotional material before you leave so that it will be there when you arrive and you will not be seen to be entering the country with it.

Intent

Many people imagine that as long as they have a visa they are guaranteed entry to a country. This is largely the case but acceptance into a country is also subject to an immigration officer's discretion. If he or she suspects that your intention is to break the terms of your visa by seeking work or that you are not intending to leave on your stated departure date you can be refused entry into the country. As long as the immigration officer is satisfied that you intend to adhere to the visa stipulations you well be able to enter.

Know your rights

It pays to know your rights when you are travelling. Not only will it help you to avoid making any accidental, visa contravening, blunders, but it will also help you to avoid being taken advantage of by officials. Each country has its own legislation when it comes to visa requirements. If you are going to be visiting a country for an extended period of time it is worth while finding out as much as you can about them either through specialist books such as in depth tour guides (like the Lonely Planet or Rough Guide travel guides) which you will be able to find in your local book store or library, or by contacting the embassy or their information service.

Passports and visas *Checklist*

✔ Check expiry date of your passport

✔ Keep photocopies of your passport information

✔ Pack extra sets of passport sized photos

✔ If you need a visa or permit make sure you are aware of the terms and conditions under which it is issued.

12
Coming home

* Back to the old routine
* Networking
* The dreaded road disease
* Being home
* Final word

> It is a change to come home off the road, after having people screaming your name, playing to a crowd of 20,000 people to your girlfriend screaming at you to help take the trash out. It's never been that hard for me, although it's always a constant 'I can't wait to get home' to 'I can't wait to get back on the road.' Learning to drive my car again is always interesting.
>
> *Dawayne Bailey (guitar: Bob Seger, Chicago).*

Adapting to life after a tour can be as challenging as touring itself. Suddenly you will go from having a tight, regimented schedule, mass media and public attention, healthy pay cheques, and having people around to pander to your every whim, to no schedule, no mass attention, no more tour salary, and having to make your own bed again. There are few professions in the

126

world which offer this degree of polarisation. It is like the anticlimax after coming home from a vacation only multiplied by a factor of 20, and requires a major adjustment to come to terms with – not just for the returning musician but also for family, friends and partners too.

'A two week adjustment period is the norm. It takes days to get used to a normal paced life after the frantic pace of touring. It takes time to re-adjust to one's mate, especially if you've been gone for awhile. It's hard to get back into doing household chores and tedious domestic duties (you mean someone doesn't just automatically pick my towels up off of the bathroom floor for me?). Your ego has been on a major high and now it's time to come down to earth with the rest of the mortals. Don't expect your relationships to feel normal immediately, and don't panic when they don't. Expect mood swings. Allot two weeks for a full decompression and you'll come out the other end fine. '
Susie Davis (keyboards: Billy Idol, Sinead O'connor, Van Morrison).

Back to your old routine or finding a new one

One of the easiest ways to ground yourself after returning from a tour is to get back into some form of routine as quickly as possible. This is particularly important if you are returning home with little or no work ahead of you and you don't have the luxury of being held on a retainer by a record company or management group (which accounts for approximately 97% of all musicians).

Networking

As soon as you get home make a point of phoning around to find out what has been happening in your absence. Even if you have only been away for a short time it is still time enough for things to change in the music industry.

Who's hiring?

If you are a freelance musician make a point of finding out who is hiring or is soon to be auditioning. Let people know about the tour you have just done as it will help reinforce that your skills are in demand.

Advice clinic with Billy Hulting

Q When the tour is over how do you adapt back to life off the road again?

A I guess the best way is to try to get into a routine. The road is so not-routine oriented when you get home it is easy to find yourself floundering and not accomplishing anything. 'What? I have to make my own bed? Cook my own food?' It isn't so bad when you know you have long breaks between tours. What I am dealing with on Lou's gig is that we travel a lot of weekend trips and are then home for three to five days before we take off again. This doesn't give you much time to have that I-just-got-back-into-town rest day. What you need to do in this sort of situation is learn to hit the ground running. As soon as you walk in the door at home you need to continue with your day as if you woke up there that morning – treat your getting home the same as if you just returned from a gig down the street. It is almost more difficult to adjust to this sort of schedule than one where you are out of town for a long time and back for a while.

Billy Hulting (percussion: Natalie Cole, Lou Rawls, Barry Manilow, Maynard Ferguson).

Agents

If you are a musician whose work is predominantly longer term (such as residencies of a month or more), use your off tour periods to find out what gigs the agents are offering. The chances are that while you have been gone they will have secured venues in other territories so it is worthwhile keeping all the agents up to date with your availability.

'One of the things I do is while on my way home I start making a list of everything I need to do or take care of, make a separate list of people you need to call. I then start on it immediately – helps me adjust to being home and getting productive.'
Billy Hulting (percussion: Natalie Cole, Lou Rawls, Barry Manilow, Maynard Ferguson).

'Lag is a bitch. It can take two weeks getting back to normal from a Japan tour. You fall asleep at 4pm ... it's a drag. Just jumping back into working as much as you can helps, letting people know you're back. Sometimes people always assume you're always out of town, so they stop calling you for gigs. So you have to get back to normal as soon as possible.'
Gene Williams (keyboards: tours: Roberta Flack, Chaka Khan, Joe).

The dreaded road disease

There are elements of a touring musician's life that are as mysterious as the spontaneous appearance of crop circles. One of them is that however many times you might tell a local venue that you are only going to be out of town for two weeks, as soon as they know you are going on tour they presume that you will never do a gig for them again. Musicians who rely on local gigs to keep them employed when they are not on tour need to avoid letting the venue know of of any prolonged impending absences.

'I think the most important thing is to not tell too many people you are leaving town, especially those who hire you a lot. We call it 'The dreaded road disease' – once they think you are on the road they just stop calling. I don't care how you tell them they just don't hear anything but 'I'm going away' which they read as 'I've decided I am leaving you – please do not call me ever again in fact, just erase my name and number from your book and forget you ever knew me – no, wait, that just isn't good enough – please act as if I never took human form on this earth because I will be out of town until I leave this planet and since I can never do another gig for you then our relationship is worthless. Forgive me but, please, do forget me.' Well – it may not be that bad but it sure seems like it some times. Maintain contact with people in town while on the road. Check your machine often enough and people won't even think you are gone. If you get called for a gig, tell them you are working that night. If they really push you and you have to tell them you are on the road tell them you will call them when you get back into town. Getting a residential 800 number will save you big money on checking your machine.
Billy Hulting (percussion: Natalie Cole, Lou Rawls, Barry Manilow, Maynard Ferguson).

'I don't know what it's like in other cities but in Los Angeles if you're not around people forget about you – except for your friends. I've noticed that people go out on the road and if you're out for any length of time and you don't stay in contact with people, when you get back it's extremely hard to plug back in and work. Most people keep checking their messages all the time and try to book gigs for when they get back – just to keep things moving smoothly.
Tim Scott (bass: Tower of Power, Stevie Wonder).

Once you are back in town make a point of contacting your regular venues and letting them know of dates you have available. It is always a good practice to make a personal connection with them every couple of months or so. Not only does it help keep you in the forefront of their memory when they are planning their gig schedule but it shows that your interested in performing there.

Advice clinic with Benny Rietveld

Q When the tour is over how do you adapt back to life off the road again?

A Get a lot of rest and don't do anything for a couple of days, just be a total bum. Then forget about the tour and start your life again.'
Benny Rietveld (bass: Santana, Sheila E, Miles Davis).

Being home

One of the first things touring musicians notice when they return home is that their homecoming is rarely how they imagined it was going to be. You may have thought that you were looking forward to going home but once it happens it can be an anti-climax. Such feelings are understandable when you consider the changes you are adapting to, moving from a frantic paced lifestyle of ego-satisfying performance to one of starkly contrasting normality. This can be hard not only for you but also for any partners and loved ones you are returning to. Although you think you have made it obvious that you are genuinely pleased to be returning to them, if they sense an underlying disappointment at your having left your road life behind it is hard for them not to take that disappointment personally. Partners often need reassurance that this is just an adjustment phase and that everything will be back to normal within a couple of weeks.

If you have been away for several weeks or more, being home can feel strangely unfamiliar. Don't be surprised if when you wake up in the middle of the night a visit to the bathroom becomes a navigational challenge. It takes a while to re-orient yourself and get used to what were once familiar surroundings. Also, expect even the most normal of tasks to feel alien. If you haven't driven for a while it will feel odd to find yourself behind the wheel again – especially if you have been travelling on the 'wrong' side of the road for any length of time.

❝ I like being home and fall into it rather quickly. The weirdest thing for me is always driving a car again, because if you've been gone for months at a time and you don't drive at all, or very rarely, if you're being driven around by people, to come back and get into your car is really strange – and just getting re-acclimatised to your house. That's another strange thing, getting back into your house or wherever you live is always strange because you haven't been there for so long. ❞
Bobby Messano (guitar: Steve Winwood, Robin Beck).

Can't wait to get back on the road

Touring can be as addictive as any drug. The chances are that even if you have just been on a tour where the PA blew up, the van broke down, and you are still waiting for your equipment or luggage to catch up with you, that you will drop everything for an opportunity to take to the road once more. There are no other professions capable of providing you with such a unique blend of pleasure, opportunity and frustration.

❝ One amazing thing is being able to be on stage, I think – personally. I mean you get to see cities and all sorts of different people and stuff, but for me it's always been just, you know, whatever your hour and a half, or two hours, or 45 minutes or whatever it is on stage is the best thing that can ever happen to anyone. ❞
Bobby Messano (guitar: Steve Winwood, Robin Beck).

All responsibilities on hold

Few people other than fellow performers ever fully appreciate the reason why 'road life' has so much appeal. Some can understand why performing in front of an audience and experiencing all the attached glamour that goes with it can hold so much fascination, but road appeal goes much further than that. It is the whole package which incorporates the performing, the travelling, communicating, and knowing that for the duration of the tour virtually all your responsibilities are put on hold.

Coming off tour means leaving the package, and all the associated caretakers behind. What can be liberating can also seem to be alarming if the tour has been long lasting. Give yourself time to adjust back to running your own life again.

❝ I love to tour – I make records so I can go on the road. Some people do it the other way around. It's gratifying to know I've been doing this since 1970. I hope I'll still be at it another 20 years … at least. ❞ *Bonnie Raitt (Bonnie Raitt Internet site).*

The final word

That there are so many artists and musicians who look forward to touring, even after having done so for 20 years or more, goes to show the extent of its appeal. It is an extraordinary way to make a living. Few other jobs are capable of instilling that much enthusiasm that far down the track. Whether you choose the short run or the long haul, life on the road is bound to leave you with a list of unforgettable experiences.

May your roadies always be good ones and your venues always be full.

'Touring is an art form. It can be destructive to family and family life, it can wreak havoc with health and relationships, but if treated with respect it can be hugely funny, rewarding, and a very life-enriching experience, and although I never quite got the balance totally right I look forward to the next one! Yee-haa! Happy touring to one and all!'
Martin Jenner (guitar: Cliff Richard, Everly Brothers).

Coming home

Checklist

✔ Give yourself time to adjust back to being home

✔ Concentrate on getting back to your normal life as quickly as possible

✔ Make a list of all the people you need to contact

✔ Network to find out what has been happening while you have been away

✔ Expect everything to feel strange for a short while

13
Pro-files

Pro-file Musician: Benny Rietveld

Instrument: bass
Tours: Santana, Sheila E, Miles Davis

How do you decide what equipment to take on the road with you?

Figure out what you actually need. Take into account which songs need what effects, which instruments, etc. Consider the type of support the tour has. If the tech support is going to be stressed (i.e. spread too thin, each crew member doing too many things), it would be better to take a set-up that is really easy to setup and maintain. Try not to take valuable, vintage, or otherwise hard-to-replace items unless you absolutely have to. Of course, this is a tough call sometimes, and everybody has to make their own choices. You may have cut that fabulous 8-bar solo in the studio on a rare '59 green Strat, but live most people just aren't going to know the difference. I try to take instruments that are really good, but are not irreplacable.

* NET *
Check Benny's web site at
www.bennyworld.com

What advice would you give anyone going on tour for the first time?

Don't overpack! You will not need half of what you think you will need. Really. Plus, you will acquire more stuff on the road.

What are the good bits about touring?

Going to places you would normally never go to. Lots of time to think about things.

What are the bad bits?

Going to places you would normally never go to. Lots of time to think about things.

What advice would you give musicians regarding contracts?

Read them ... thoroughly. If you can't understand the lingo, get an impartial third party to help you.

How do you deal with living at such close quarters with fellow band members?

In my case, in the Santana band, most of us have known each other awhile, and we're all pretty good friends. If it's a case where you're just thrown together with a bunch of other people

Benny rehearsing twith Santana

you don't know, then it becomes an exercise in learning to get along with strangers. Eventually you find the common ground between everybody, and you can interact with them on those levels. It's just like the rest of life – everybody's different, so cut each other some slack, okay? Make a little extra effort to understand the other person's ways.

How do you amuse yourself/ stop yourself from going insane on the road?

Watch movies or read books that I normally wouldn't have time for at home. Write music. Do or learn something else! Kenny Garrett (sax player in the Miles Davis band) took it upon himself to learn Japanese on the road. He was always practicing, listening to the tapes, etc.

Besides your gear what personal stuff do you take on the road for entertainment or its comfort value?

A book, a couple of magazines.

What's the worst/funniest/most memorable thing that has happened to you on the road? Have you ever experienced any memorable cultural problems touring overseas?

Only that I clapped for Miles during the ceremony where they named him a Knight Of Malta, somewhere in Spain. Everybody turned and looked at me quite sternly, since it was in some palace and supposed to be a real 'dignified' event.

When the tour is over how do you adapt back to life off the road again?

Get a lot of rest and don't do anything for a couple of days, just be a total bum. Then forget about the tour and start your life again.

TIP
When the tour is over, get a lot of rest and don't do anything for a couple of days, just be a total bum.

What has been the most alarming technical problem you have experienced on stage?

In Sheila E's band, after doing a dance step (a split), my pants ripped open slightly, right at the crotch area. I wasn't wearing any underwear, so I suddenly felt air on my genitalia. I was exposing myself to thousands of people at the Superdome in New Orleans! I had a wireless, so I danced offstage, still playing, and the wardrobe girl had to put a spare pair of pants on me while I was playing... It was very amusing...

Pro-file Musician/ artist: Billy Hulting

✻ NET ✻

Billy's web site is at
www.zerobpm.com/billy/

Instruments: percussion
Tours: Lou Rawls, Natalie Cole, Barry Manilow, Maynard Ferguson.

What is the first thing you do when you get the phone call inviting you to join a tour?

Celebrate – it isn't easy to get a tour. Next thing is to get confirmed dates from the management company. You need to cover any gigs you will miss while out of town. If they can't give you a confirmation on a gig don't sub the in-town gig out yet. Nothing is that solid – especially these days – so don't pass on any gigs until you have been promised dates. Once they promise dates to you you have more weight on your side as far as being compensated in case the gig they gave you falls through and you have subbed out or turned down gigs in town. There is also an art to negotiating your deal. Most tours seem to just have a set rate – take it or leave it – so there isn't much you can do. Sometimes, however, there is the possibility for negotiating.

How do you decide what gear to take?

Now I don't take any more than I need to do the gig the best I can. This will differ from gig to gig. If you have techs out who will be setting up your gear you can make them very unhappy by bringing a lot of stuff out with you that you really just don't need. Sure – you want your setup to look cool (especially true for drummers and percussionists) but you really don't want to hang the guys up too much. I'm sure if the techs for Natalie Cole read this they'll be laughing – I used this huge cage with everything hanging on it – eight cymbals, drumKAT and malletKAT with loads of external triggers and stuff. I used it all and believe it was very effective – Natalie's gig covered a lot of musical territory. She also did a good number of ballads and I felt the artistic need to make the percussion parts a little different on each so I think the large set-up was justified. Big racks for percussionists were just coming into style then – I used to tell Natalie that every star as big as she deserved to have a percussionist with a really cool setup!

With Lou we rent almost everything. I bring a trap case with a cymbal stand/percussion tree and some hand toys. The case, loaded, weighs 68&1/2 lbs. – 70lbs is the limit for normal baggage on airplanes – we fly everywhere so it needs to be that weight to avoid 'excess' charges.

How do you protect your gear?

Big truck tours – get a hard ATA approved flight case. Gear just gets worn out and beat up on tour – it can't be avoided but the process can be slowed. Any compromise in selecting cases will have a direct effect on the safety of your gear.

Do you do a maintenance check on everything before going on tour?

If we didn't have rehearsals going straight into the tour I might set up the electronics and give them a run through. Most of the tours I've done have had great techs so they could catch anything immediately and fix it even during a show. On Barry's gig Dave Benson had it worked out so that he could reload the memory of any electronic unit on stage while we were playing and we had three keyboard players in addition to my drumKat and malletKAT setups as well as a drummer who was playing all pads. He was amazing. The first tech I had for Natalie was David Hackbarth – he could hardwire any broken unit to work. Once I left my Cable trunk at home and with a few rag-tag pieces he managed to not only cable and set pedals for everything but hard wired my malletKAT modules together. Brent Jeffers was the second tech I had with Natalie – once when my malletKAT memory dumped due to a power surge he managed to help me reprogram it during a show – the song coming up was "Live For Your Love" which I started by playing the sequenced keyboard part. If we hadn't gotten it re-programed the show would have stopped dead. Your techs should be your best friends on the road – buy them drinks often – let them date your sister.

✳ TIP ✳
Your techs should be your best friends on the road – buy them drinks often – let them date your sister.

What information does the artist's manager/tour manager want from you?

Social Security numbers, passport information, a list of cases you will be bringing. You only need a detailed list of your gear (serial numbers and all) if you are traveling out of the country for the manifest the show to customs. You also need to let them know about any special needs – Non-smoking rooms, for example. Also – any special diet requirements for when you are getting a catered meal. On Lou's gig Curtis (bass player) and I have a vegan diet – Lou's Tour Manager, John Molinare, had us print up a vegan menu for him to fax ahead to the promoter for the gigs which provide dinner. He also sent a list of our frequent flyer numbers, preferred seats, and special meal requests to the travel agent so they can enter the info in while booking our flights- what a guy!

What advice would you give anyone going on tour for the first time?

There is so much – I think the most important thing is to not tell too many people you are leaving town especially those who hire you a lot. We call it 'The Dreaded Road Disease' – once they think you are on the road they just stop calling. I don't care how you tell them they just don't hear anything but 'I'm going away' which they read as 'I've decided I am leaving you – please do not call me ever again in fact, just erase my name and number from your book and forget you ever knew me – no, wait, that just isn't good enough – please act as if I never took human form on this earth because I will be out of town until I leave this planet and since I can never do another gig for you then our relationship is worthless. Forgive me but, please, do forget me.' Well – it may not be that bad but it sure seems like it some times. Maintain contact with people in town while on the road. Check your machine often enough and people won't even think you are gone. If you get called for a gig tell them you are working that night. If they really push you and you have to tell them you are on the road tell them you will call them when you get back into town. Getting a residential 800 number will save you big money on checking your machine.

What are the good bits about touring?

Travel and people. I am fascinated by people and how they interact. When you travel extensively you get to see a lot of different situations and you get to see a lot of similar situations just acted out by different people. I think it helps with your basic understanding of your own life.

What are the bad bits?

There are quite a few – early leave times from hotels, bad rental gear, two shows in one day separated by three hours, bad information from hotel employees, screaming babies on planes, late flights, screaming babies on delayed flights after an early leave, not being at home. There are all sorts of quirky weird things to deal with BUT – the way to stay sane is to realize you are making a living playing an instrument – PLAYING is the key word here. Maynard Fergusson used to say 'I never went to work a day in my life – I always went to play.' If you believe in luck – you are lucky to not only be playing but lucky that you landed a tour.

How do you amuse yourself/ stop yourself from going insane on the road?

Believe it or not – the road gets very boring. There is so much waiting and sitting around you can let it get to you. It can very easily cause you to turn dark about your situation. At first we just drank a lot – go out trying to meet girls. Sure we still do that but I seem to drink less.

Exercise, – even a little. Get out of the room. More often than not you will find yourself watching 'Spies Like Us' every weekend out on the road. The television is a powerful thing in that hotel room. There is a lot of great programming out there now but on the road you may often find you turn towards the junk or things you have seen countless times – probably the comfort of familiarity. Go for a walk or something. I work out a lot at home so I try to continue it on the road. I carry a bag with my in-line skates during the Summer – great way to see a place and get some exercise.

✳ ✳ ✳
✳ **TIP** ✳
Exercise, – even a little.
Get out of the room.

Besides your gear what personal stuff do you take on the road for entertainment or its comfort value?

I carry a Mac Powerbook with me so I can be very productive. I can stay in touch with friends via e-mail, work with Finale toy get charts ready, ear training, type letters. I even learned how to design a web page while riding in a van on the way to a gig. Great for staying sane. I need to feel like I'm accomplishing something all the time. The Powerbook is a dream for that. I also read a lot. I hardly ever find the time to read at home but on the road I have a lot of time. I've really started educating myself in several subjects just because I can actually take the time to read because I'm out of town.

There is also a lot of time to listen and study music. On Barry's gig I brought two speakers for my walkman and after every show I would go to my room and listen to Parliament Funkadelic so I wouldn't lose my groove. Playing Barry's music was cool but there wasn't much in the way of the heavy groove stuff.

If you are going to take a CD player or Walkman – don't spend too much money – it will get beat up. Take something that you like that won't break your budget.

What's the worst thing that has happened to you on the road?

Let's see – hmmm – the bus which almost slipped off a cliff in Colorado?... no ... my gear overheating at the Playboy Jazz Festival at the Hollywood Bowl?... no ... Pam telling me she was seeing someone else?... Almost getting beat up by racists in Ohio?... no ... I've got it! On our way to Jakarta, Indonesia, my passport was lost/stolen on the plane. I say lost/stolen because I had left it on the plane when we stopped in Singapore to make a change and by the time I was allowed back on to look for it it had been taken. I couldn't get on the connecting flight so I was forced to wait in the airport until it could be located. Well – no such luck. I had to spend the night in the Singapore airport. Morning – still no word. I still had until that evening to get to the first show in Jakarta. Well, the US embassy was closed for a holiday so I was going to miss the show that night. I did, however, get Singapore immigration to release me into the city, unchaperoned, overnight with absolutely no identification. Cool, huh? I did get a new passport and work visa (imagine me not having changed clothes in two days, with long hair and earrings walking into the consulate of a Muslim country asking for a replacement for a work visa for which I didn't have the complete paperwork) and arrived at the venue in Jakarta twenty minutes before the first set. It seems almost funny now but it certainly wasn't then nor for many months to follow. I tell you – since then I have been in some tough and weird situations but they just don't bother me anymore.

What's the best thing that's happened on tour?
Some of the concert halls I've soloed in – Suntory Hall in Japan, Philharmonic Hall in Berlin in front of twenty million T.V. Viewers at the Berlin Jazz Festival – they were great. Meeting and hanging with some great players after a gig we shared the bill on.

What advice would you give musicians regarding contracts?
I never signed a contract for a tour – Barry had the closest thing which was a letter of intent. I scratched off a lot of stuff, signed only what I wanted to, and turned it back in. Not much was said.

Mostly you have what is referred to as a deal. You agree on a pay schedule and per diem and that's really all. Some of the super huge tours may have a retainer or contracts. One good thing to agree on is some sort of separation clause. Two weeks notice for cancellations. If they come under that two week thing then you should get paid. You also need to give them two weeks notice before you want to leave. They may hate the thought of this but it really benefits you both. If they argue against it ,(I had one management company try,) just tell them that by their own definition you could show up at the airport and tell them you aren't going – that ought to switch them to your side.

When the tour is over how do you adapt back to life off the road again?

I guess the best way is to try to get into a routine. The road is so not-routine oriented when you get home it is easy to find yourself floundering and not accomplishing anything. 'What I have to make my own bed? Cook my own food? It isn't so bad when you know you have long breaks between tours. What I am dealing with on Lou's gig is that we travel a lot of weekend trips and are then home for three to five days before we take off again. This doesn't give you much time to have that I-Just-got-back-into-town rest day. What you need to do in this sort of situation is learn to hit the ground running. As soon as you walk in the door at home you need to continue with your day as if you woke up there that morning, treat your getting home the same as if you just returned from a gig down the street. It ís almost more difficult to adjust to this sort of schedule than one where you are out of town for a long time and back for a while.

One of the things I do is while on my way home I start making a list of everything I need to do or take care of, make a separate list of people you need to call. I then start on it immediately – helps me adjust to being home and getting productive.

There are a lot of little things I have learned over the years – they may seem trite or silly but you'd be surprised at what a difference they make. Always have aspirin handy. Carry it in your carry on luggage. Days can turn ugly fast so it will help to keep some handy. Also, carry contact lens solution or re-wetting drops, especially on planes.

Condoms – when you first get on the road you will be overwhelmed with this new power you have. Everyone notices it but few like to talk about it or admit it. Be prepared. You will immediately be more attractive to potential sexual partners then you were before.

Take something to practice on. Guitar and bass players can get those personal headphone amps and practice anywhere. It ís harder for keyboard players. Drummers and percussionists can bring a pad. It may not seem like much but it will help. It is easy to develop road chops from playing the same music or show over and over again. You will find you can still play that stuff well but other areas of your playing, technically and musically, will suffer – that is what we call road chops.

✳ TIP ✳
One of the things I do is while on my way home I start making a list of everything I need to do or take care of, make a separate list of people you need to call. I then start on it immediately – helps me adjust to being home and getting productive.

Pro-file Musician: Bobby Messano

Instrument: guitar
Tours: Steve Winwood, Robin Beck

One of the things I have learned, which is really strange, about being on the road is that everybody tends to go out on the road, and sort of go berserk – especially the first times they've been out. One of the best things you can do is sleep and eat well, would you believe? What ends up happening is that within a really short period of time, no matter what you're doing – it's very difficult to deal with things if you're not sleeping well. One of the things I've definitely done ... on planes and tour buses I've always just tried to sleep as much as is humanly possible. It actually takes the edge off and makes your days go a lot quicker.

How do you cope with living at close quarters to other band members?

Well, um ... dependent upon what you're doing – if you're busing it, you just sort of get used to it and you decide who you want to be near and who you don't want to be near. (Laughs) And if you're on a big tour you usually have the luxury of being able to have your own hotel room, more likely than not.

Does every tour have its own pain in the butt?

Absolutely, and you usually turn to your road manager or your tour manager and say 'please – I can't take this person,' and let them take care of it. It's very strange, especially being thrown into a situation with people you don't know at all, and you have to cultivate relationships rather quickly.

What are the good bits?

One amazing thing is being able to be on stage, I think, – personally. I mean you get to see cities and all sorts of different people and stuff, but for me it's always been just, you know, whatever your hour and a half, or two hours, or forty-five minutes or whatever it is on stage is the best thing that can ever happen to anyone.

What's the worst thing that's happened to you on stage?

When I was with Steve Winwood we were playing in Berlin – and outdoor show in this beautiful garden setting, in front of six or seven thousand people there. And my guitar tech didn't realise that we were going on stage at the time that we were going on stage, and as the band started walking up the stairs to the stage he realised that all of my guitars were detuned, and I picked one up and walked onto the stage with it and the strings were flapping. And it opened up with a guitar solo. So, needless to say nothing really happened. I was trying to tune while the song was going on and … that was one interesting event.

Another one was I was touring with Robin Beck in Germany and it was the second to last show we did there, in Nurenberg – or some place, and my rack equipment sort of decided to go on fire. We actually had to stop the show for ten minutes while we put the flames out, figured out what was the matter and got me playing again, because I was the main guitar player on the tour … and one other time I was tripped on a stage and I slid across the entire stage and landed on the monitor desk. It was embarrassing I just sort of stayed on my back on the stage and finished the song.

I did a show where I had a problem with my eye – where someone had stuck their thumb in my eye – I had a patch on so I couldn't really see and the lights were blinding me and every time I would get near the front of the stage one of the roadies would come on and move me back. You get used to these things.

Have you ever had a really bad sound systems to deal with?
Periodically I've had bad systems, more when you're an opening act but most of the tours I've done have had brilliant sound systems, and great monitors and everything because they usually travel with you.

When you've had a bad sound system what have you been able to do about it?
Most of those situations fall into the opening act category where you might not get monitors or they might not want to help you out, or anything, so you just have to go and play and not have an attitude. That's really important, if you're in a situation like that and you cop some kind of very strange attitude or if you're not nice to the crew or something, you're gonna pay for it. You will be punished.

Have you ever had problems with power leakages?
I'm always wireless. I haven't had a corded guitar system for fifteen years. I've had a couple of really bad incidents of pseudo electrocution. I was knocked out once on stage by a bad ground, and I ended up on the floor completely knocked out with my guitar on top of me, with my gums bleeding. 'Cos someone cut a ground someplace and no one realised it. All I saw was a big spark and that was the end of time for a few minutes.

✳ ✳ ✳
✳ **TIP** ✳
'I'm always wireless. I haven't had a corded guitar system for fifteen years.'

Do you have circuit breakers set into your gear?
If you're wireless nothing will happen.

Have you had any bad experiences with immigration when you've been going into other countries?
Personally I've had no problems at all.

What about cultural problems?
Only in France. They were sort of not happy because I was American and I did one of those faux pas of ordering like a ham and shoe sandwich or something – they sort of laughed and it was like you're a stupid American and you're in our country. Everyone I know who's been there lately say it's much better now though.

How do you stop yourself from going insane while you're on the road?
I don't know – thousands of dollars in phone calls? A couple of things work for me. One is sightseeing, whenever you get the chance. It's sort of neat to see the city and get a feel for the place, and if you've been there before you know what to look for and what not to look for. The other thing is when I'm on a tour I read a lot of books. And shopping always works. If you have any extra money shopping does work. Take your per diems and go shopping.

Do you take anything on the road with you for entertainment?
No, just a CD Player and a Cassette deck. Some of the tours I've been on they set up a little room with a four-track or eight-track if you felt like writing, or something, which was sort of neat. I always have a micro cassette recorder. I write a lot. I'll always have that with me so I can write something real quick and throw it on a micro cassette.

How do you cope with living in hotels and what sort of things annoy you?
The only thing that really annoys me in hotels is making phone calls because if you don't have some kind of phone credit card then they're gonna harass you with taxes. But I'm so used to living in hotels that it doesn't bother me. One of the carry-overs from doing big tours, for me, is that I really like nice hotels. It's not very cost effective but I still would rather stay in a Hilton or Hyatt. I'd rather be in one of those than a dinky horrible ... but

other than that you just get sort of used to it after a while. It can be lonely, but if that's what you do, it's no different from being a salesman, or something, you're always spending your time in hotels so you just have to try and make the best of it and be in as nice a place as you can – hopefully paid for by someone else.

Musicians are notorious for practical joking. Do you find a lot of that happens on tours?

The last night of any tour, – that is the night for the complete and maniacal practical joking. Drummers walk out on stage and not realising it hit their snare and have baby powder on the snare – it's light so you can't see it until they hit it and have the stuff flying all over them; and had the sticks cut half way through, so they break. I've seen techs super-glued to everything. Then you go try to pull a pick off the stand or off the top of your amps or racks, or something and it won't come off because it's super-glued.

When we were with Winwood, the last night of the tour we crazy-stringed him – every single person in the band and crew, which is probably twenty, or twenty-five people all had a can of crazy string, and there was a monstrous crazy-string person on the stage.

I had myself duct taped. I was doing a guitar solo alone and there were like seven or eight spotlights on me, and the crew ran out, tucked my arms behind my back and duct taped my arms and laid me on the ground with those spotlights on me as someone else behind my amps played the guitar solo. I know of other uses of duct tape but I try not to go into them.. It's pretty strange. I had a fish thrown over my head from the back of an amp stack once – I mean, on a fishing pole. It was withdrawn on the fishing pole and hit me on the head. It was an actual fish, it wasn't like a plastic fish. A lot of strange stuff goes on.

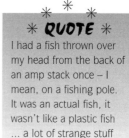

✳ QUOTE ✳
I had a fish thrown over my head from the back of an amp stack once – I mean, on a fishing pole. It was an actual fish, it wasn't like a plastic fish … a lot of strange stuff goes on.

How do you adjust to life off the tour when you come home?

I like being home and fall into it rather quickly. The weirdest thing for me is always driving a car again, because if you've been gone for months at a time and you don't drive at all, or very rarely, if you're being driven around by people, to come back and get into your car is really strange – and just getting re-aclimated to your house. That's another strange thing, getting back into your house or wherever you live is always strange because you haven't been there for so long.

Pro-file Musician: Carol Kaye

Instrument: bass guitar
Track record: Session Musician on Richi Valens 'La Bamba', Beach Boys hits.
Tours: Hampton Hawes

How do you decide what equipment to take on the road with you?

It depends on the types of music you're playing, usually the roadie takes care of it. You want to make sure you have good hard traveling cases though and I always carried my bass in a gig bag on board the plane where they put it in the coat closet, or it usually fit in the overhead bin. Back in the 50s, we traveled by car and the band truck carried everything.

What advice would you give anyone going on tour for the first time?

Be sure to eat right on your first road trip, take along a good book, don't use drugs, be on time at all costs, keep track of your packing, your instrument(s) at all times, make lists every day of traveling. Keep a relaxed attitude tho' once you got all accounted for, don't let yourself get uptight.

What are the good bits about touring?

Seeing all kinds of people, all the tourist things, the fun of traveling can be good if the airlines are good, the connections are good the accommodations are good, eating out is fun if you find lots of good places.

What are the bad bits?

You get tired quickly, bored, and if you don't exercise every day you get in bad shape fast with all the stress of traveling. Sometimes the fans are little too weird too, be careful, but mostly the people do express appreciation and that's always nice.

How do you amuse yourself/ stop yourself from going insane on the road?

Read upbeat books, keep upbeat thoughts, don't insist on everything being 'your way,' take a team spirit and be part of a team, you're all going to the same place, all playing together, so treat the job for the job it is: something you all do together, and pull together for the best of the job. Get a hobby (like bowling, guys even like to crochet, reading, etc.,) something you can do on the road that is totally different than music. The TV shows musicians always 'jamming' while on the road, believe me, I think this is a fallacy. You take the time to get away from music, to enjoy other things – this makes your music then fresher when you do play.

Besides your gear what personal stuff do you take on the road for entertainment or its comfort value?
Books, a portable hobby of some sort, instead of laying down watching the TV all the time.

What's the worst/funniest/most memorable thing that has happened to you on the road?
I was helping my bass-player husband (we were on the road with a big pop dance-band, he played string bass and I was the guitarist in 1955) do his model boats in Lakeland Florida. There wasn't much town there then, and it was lovely, we noticed all the beautiful lakes, just perfect for running the model boats on a string. I was out waist-deep in the lake and letting the boat run around me on the string when I felt something brush against me, it felt like a log. Then about twenty to thirty feet away shortly after, there was a boat with 2 men on it pulling up a huge alligator out of this lake I was standing in. My husband laughed as I scrambled out of this lake, no-one told us they all had alligators in them. Uh-uh, he could run his own damn boats after that.

Another one, we were playing at the Memphis Peabody Hotel. It was so windy on the roof of that hotel (we played there in addition to the main room downstairs) that during the live radio broadcast (coast to coast) we'd do, the two sax players in front would be playing and their right hands would come up to hold their toupees down in unison, the rhythm section would laugh. This probably doesn't sound so funny these days, but it was hilarious then.

Is gigging today different from how it was when you first started out as a musician?
You travel more by plane now. Artie Shaw and I were discussing traveling during those times vs. traveling now (we talk sometimes on the phone, he's a grand older man) and it seems that it was harder then, all the car travel, setting up, not much sleep, but the gigs felt exactly the same once you started playing. (I traveled in the early and mid 50s a lot, and then again in the middle 70s).

✳ QUOTE ✳
Artie Shaw and I were discussing traveling during those times vs. traveling now ... and it seems that it was harder then, all the car travel, setting up, not much sleep, but the gigs felt exactly the same once you started playing.

✳ NET ✳
Dawayne's web site is at
www.geocities.com/Holly
wood/Boulevard/3391

Pro-file Musician: Dawayne Bailey

Instrument: guitar
Tours: Bob Seger, Chicago

How do you decide what equipment to take on the road with you?

I always take gear that will cover the specified job. And as less as possible, but I always have backup gear for immediate change in case of breakdowns, etc. I've played a lot of outdoor concerts and I've seen rainstorms destroy gear, so you always have to be prepared for the unexpected and bring at least two of everything.

How do you deal with living at such close quarters with fellow band members?

Living in close quarters with others on 10-18 hour bus rides, sometimes 24 hour rides, can and will be tiring, tedious, and sometimes downright obnoxious and overbearing. Try not to do drugs, get plenty of sleep and exercise. Eat healthy and have an amazing amount of patience and a sense of humor goes a *long* way too.

What advice would you give anyone going on tour for the first time?

Advice for first-timers would be to not go overboard with long distance phone calls, partying too much, try not to burn your bridges with other people on the crew, in the band, and with your audience. Keep a positive attitude and try to save your money, and bring protection for those romantic interludes.

What are the good bits about touring?

The good bits? Playing to audiences around the world, meeting new people, seeing new places, trying new cultures and food, expanding your life experiences in general.

What are the bad bits?

Missing out on your friends and families' personal events like birthdays, graduations, funerals, get-togethers. Living a 'normal' life, spending most of your time traveling just to be able to play music on stage for only a couple of hours.

How do you amuse yourself/ stop yourself from going insane on the road?

I bring a bicycle, books, magazines, video cameras, Walkman tape recorders and plenty of my 'home tapes' of favorite music to listen to, videos, and a small mini-studio for recording ideas on the bus or in the hotel room, all help curb insanity.

What's the worst/funniest/most memorable thing that has happened to you on the road?

Worst-funniest-memorable moment? Getting arrested and thrown in jail for being too young while playing in a club in Oklahoma; accidentally letting a crazed audience member grab my guitar and having it all start a riot where people got hurt and I could have been sued; the end of a tour when the crew and band give each other some big surprises – such as the crew dropping hundreds of fish from above the stage onto the band; playing in your hometown with all of your old friends and family there to cheer you on. I could go on and on.

Have you ever experienced any memorable cultural problems touring overseas?

The main cultural problem is just making sure you don't offend too many people in distinctively different places like Thailand, or really anywhere for that matter, with dumb behaviour or just being a "rude American" – I've never experienced any problems personally, but I've seen people get over zealous and offend the natives.

When the tour is over how do you adapt back to life off the road again?

It is a change to come home off the road, after having people screaming your name, playing to a crowd of 20,000 people to your girlfriend screaming at you to help take the trash out. It's never been that hard for me, although it's always a constant 'I can't wait to get home' to 'I can't wait to get back on the road'. Learning to drive my car again is always interesting.

Is gigging today different from how it was when you first started out as a musician?

Gigging today is very different. Buses are better equipped and safer. Gear in general works better and is better designed. Promoters are more scrutinized and don't screw the bands over as much. There's more concentration on the music than throwing TV's out of hotel windows, more of a disease scare so the wild sex orgies aren't as stupid and rampant, there's more competition so the music and sound systems are much better. Musicians have hopefully learned to not burn out before their time and bring their families on the road to create a more 'normal' lifestyle while touring.

Pro-file Musician: Gene Williams

Instrument: keyboards
Tours: Roberta Flack, Chaka Khan, Joe

How do you decide what equipment to take on the road with you?

Well, I rarely take my own equipment on the road. I usually have them rent the gear I want to use. Because I work with different artists, I tend to use different keyboards for a given project ... For example, when I work with an artist named Saundra St. Victor, I'm the only keyboardist, and my role in her band requires me to use a Fender Rhodes, Korg o1w, and a Korg Trinity. Now, on the Joe Tour, my role is as the secondary keyboardist, so I have a Roland xp80, Roland jd800, and a Korg o1w put on the tech rider. So it depends on the sounds I'm required to produce, and finding the instruments that can best reproduce the original sounds used on the artists album.

I'm usually required to play strings, so I tend to lean toward using proteus strings midi-ed with either an 01w or an XP80 ... but I like to experiment, so it can be different every time.

What advice would you give anyone going on tour for the first time?

When touring internationally I'm always most concerned with representing myself in the best way possible. I go to Japan often and I've seen how easy it can be to offend someone because you didn't understand the different culture. So respecting others (including your band mates) would be my main bit of advice. Don't let egos and bad attitudes come into play, you may find yourself being sent back home on the bus alone and replaced in the middle of the tour. Remember, the tour group will be your extended family for a week, month, or even longer. So there's no room for bad vibes.

And be on time. It's a drag waiting around for people that have no consideration for other peoples' time and are always late. I don't care how great a player you are, If you get a bad reputation for always being late, you're gonna stop getting called for gigs.

How do you deal with living at such close quarters with fellow band members?

Well, right now I'm on a bus with about nine other people. It's a pretty big bus so it's not too bad. I'm used to flying, this is my first bus tour after being in this business for about ten years. I've known a few of these people for years, that helps. It helps when

* ✳ ✳
✳ **QUOTE** ✳
Remember, the tour group will be your extended family for a week, month, or even longer. So there's no room for bad vibes.

you've got a lot in common. Even though this is an r&b tour most of the people on this bus are fusion heads. We're having a ball listening to old Mahavishnu, Miles, and Herbie, and we're watching some great movies like 'Goodfellas' and 'Star Wars.' Two of us have laptop computers, another guy brought a Sony Play station, another guy sleeps all the time. This is still early on in the tour but so far we're having a lot of fun together. Ask me again a month from now.

Besides your gear what personal stuff do you take on the road for entertainment or its comfort value?
I try not to take too much stuff with me these days. It's a drag moving it all around. And the gear, – someone else moves it for me. Traveling light is the way to go. We all share everything, so it's all good.

What's the worst/funniest/most memorable thing that has happened to you on the road?
Hmmm ... would have to be the time in Japan when a local band asked me to stay to see their performance and after waiting in the club two hours for the set to start, they came on wearing black faces and Afro wigs. They didn't do it as an insult ... but I was so mad I left the club after their first song. A week later they saw me and asked me what I thought of their gig. I told them I respected them as musicians, but in the U.S. wearing black face is an insult to African Americans. I wasn't sure if they understood due to the obvious language barrier, but a week later I was again invited to their next show, and was happy to see they no longer wore the black face make up.

When the tour is over how do you adapt back to life off the road again?
Lag is a bitch. It can take two weeks getting back to normal from a Japan tour. You fall asleep at 4pm ... it's a drag. Just jumping back into working as much as you can helps. Letting people know your back. Sometimes people always assume you're always out of town, so they stop calling you for gigs. So you have to get back to normal as soon as possible.

✳ **QUOTE** ✳
Lag is a bitch. It can take two weeks getting back to normal from a Japan tour.

Is gigging today different from how it was when you first started out as a musician?
The gigs are still the same, it's my approach to them that's different. I don't stress over little things any more. It's only music. I know what I'm doing ... so does everyone else. I'm still having fun whether it's a club date, theater, TV or stadium. It's what I do. It's all good!

Pro-file Musician: Julie Homi

Instrument: piano, keyboards
Tours: Robert Palmer, Yanni, Peter Cetera

What's the first thing you do when you get the phone call inviting you to join a tour?

I try to get some basic information, such as: what are the projected dates of the tour (and rehearsal period)? Where is the tour going? What sized venues are they playing? (This gives me an idea of what conditions and salary I can expect.) Will they be touring by bus, plane, or both? Usually, I do more listening than talking during the first conversation, letting the manager (or tour manager or musical director) give me as much information as they want to. If they are clear about the actual work they are offering, and if we both feel I would be suitable for the gig, then I will go on to the next step. I offer to send a package (resume, video, photo), which I do promptly, the same day if possible, by Express mail. If they're scheduling auditions, we will discuss the details of those. They will usually send me CDs or tapes of the songs I'm expected to learn. If they won't give me solid details about the tour, and they throw out a lot of vague 'pie in the sky' talk about possible future work, my bullshit antennae go up. This is probably not a serious offer. During the first conversation, I try to sound cheerful and interested. I don't ask too many questions – I wait and see if I get the gig first.

How do you decide what gear to take?

This varies considerably between tours, and is usually decided during the rehearsal period. A few factors are involved: what are the musical requirements of the gig? Am I providing a lot of big, fat MIDI layered sounds, or am I just covering piano and organ? Are there space restrictions? If we have a couple of semis for the gear, I can take as much as I want, but if we're checking equipment on passenger planes, I might have to scale down considerably. Sometimes, the artist tells me what he/she wants me to take, occasionally providing some or all of it. In other situations, some gear is rented, and I just bring a small rack.

How do you protect your gear?

I buy good-quality, custom-made cases, with reinforced corners. I make sure I go over with my tech exactly how my gear will be packed, where accessories will be stored, and we stuff any dead space with foam or toweling. I make sure every piece has my

Stadium eye-view for Julie Homi

name stenciled on it. I carry my own musical instrument insurance, in addition to any insurance the tour may carry.

What advice would you give to anyone going on tour for the first time?

Be considerate of the crew, not demanding. Remember that however exhausted you may feel on the road, they work much longer, harder hours and probably feel ten times worse. Avoid becoming romantically or sexually involved with anyone in the organization. This is much easier said than done. The road can be a lonely place, and most of us want to cuddle up with someone at the end of the night. However, it is far safer to make new friends along the way (or fly old ones in) than to complicate your professional life with personal entanglements. Don't complain too much, especially at first. If you do complain, try and do it with a sense of humor. It will be better received.

What advice would you give a female musician about life on the road?

The recommendation to avoid sexual involvements with co-workers holds especially true for women. Often, a woman is in the minority on a tour, and jealousy and resentment can develop if she starts shacking up with one of the guys. I find it safer to think of myself as one of the guys, or maybe their sister. I don't mind doing a little mothering now and then, as long as they don't take it for granted. I recommend tolerance: let boys be boys.

How would you describe life on the road?

Life on the road is full of paradoxes. It's complicated, because a large group of people are mounting a sophisticated production in a different town almost every night, yet it's simple, because as a band member, all I have to do is be in the hotel lobby when the tour manager tells me to. Everything else is taken care of. I am transported, fed, provided with a place to sleep at night and a wake-up call in the morning. My luggage is carried for me, my gear is set-up on stage.

Life on the road can be lonely, especially on a long tour, but it can be very social, also a great opportunity to hook up with good friends I hardly ever see, make new friends, or even live out my fantasies with musical admirers (that's politically correct for groupies). A strong connection can develop with others in the group, and sometimes lasting friendships are formed. When a good tour ends, my feelings are bittersweet. I'm ready to go home, yet there is regret about leaving the group, who have come to feel like my family. The road is tedious and predictable, yet full of surprises. It's glamorous one minute and uncomfortable the next. You can be the toast of the town one place and unable to fill the house in another.

What are the good bits?

Enthusiastic audiences, getting paid to travel to exotic places, seeing old friends, being treated like a celebrity, road romances , days off, watching videos in the back lounge of the bus, meeting celebrities, knowing I did a great show that night.

What are the bad bits?

Waiting around in lobbies and airport lounges, long soundchecks, playing eighteen straight shows without a day off, travel days, meeting someone you like in a town, and having to get on the bus and leave them after the show.

How do you amuse yourself/ stop yourself from going insane on the road?

I laugh a lot. Every tour I've done has its own store of private jokes , and I try to contribute as much as I can. I like getting to the point where I'm laughing so hard, I'm afraid I might have an accident. It reminds me of summer camp. Some tours have a newsletter, which usually has a humorous bent, and I like to contribute to those, too. I have shot comedy videos about the tour. This was a great creative outlet for me, and a source of entertainment and embarrassment for others. One video became so ambitious, I missed soundcheck once because I was filming a scene. I don't recommend that. I call friends at home regularly. Life on the road can get very insular, and it is important to remind myself that I have another life waiting for me when the tour ends.

How do you travel? Have you always been in a tour bus situation with all the musicians together or had to travel on your own?

I have traveled by myself, with 90 people, and several other sized groups in between. My favorite situation is a medium sized group of 15 to 25 people. I find traveling on a tour bus less exhausting than flying on planes.

Besides your gear what personal stuff do you take on the road for entertainment or its comfort value?

Sometimes, I take a teddy bear. I take spiritual books and a few favorite CDs, sentimental photos, my work-out gear, maybe a comedy video or tape to share with the group.

What's the worst thing that has happened to you on the road?

I have been lucky. I have never experienced a real touring nightmare. One of the scariest memories I have is this: the band was doing a vocal rehearsal in the artist's hotel room, and the phone rang. It was the president of the record company, threatening to bring us home the next day from a tour that was supposed to last another month. I sat in silence, my stomach in knots, as I listened to my boss persuade the record exec. to let us finish the tour. Luckily, he succeeded.

The best thing that's happened on tour.

My father, who had never seen me perform professionally, flew in to spend a couple of days with me on tour. He watched a rehearsal and two shows, and he was very impressed with the whole thing. He confessed that he'd never considered what I did a real job, and he had no idea I worked so hard. It was very validating for me to have him see me in such a professional situation. Everyone made a fuss of him and he had his picture taken with some celebrities. He had a really good time, and it meant a lot to me.

Pro-file Musician: Kevin Dukes

Instrument: guitar
Tours: Boz Scaggs, Don Henley, Jackson Browne

What is the first thing you do when you get the phone call inviting you to join a tour?
Determine the length of obligation, salary and payment specifics.

How do you decide what gear to take?
The style and range of styles of the music involved and the size of the crew and venues dictate what's appropriate.

What advice would you give anyone going on tour for the first time?
Make yourself comfortable. Find a way to stay in touch with friends and family on a frequent basis. Find a way to continue religious practice, and make a point to keep up hobbies and exercise routines. Otherwise you fall into the common tendency of developing the 'road' persona and the 'home' persona and going through periods of decompression transitioning from one to the other.

What are the bad bits?
Living in such an ungrounded transient state for extended periods of time.

How do you amuse yourself/ stop yourself from going insane on the road?
At one point I played golf regularly. Now I have a road case for my mountain bike and I have seen places I've been dozens of times in a completely new light, plus have the added benefit of being able to exercise outdoors and burn off road steam.

Besides your gear what personal stuff do you take on the road for entertainment or its comfort value?
I have taken pillows, recording gear, golf clubs, books, but now it's primarily my bike.

What's the worst thing that has happened to you on the road?
A hellish example was finishing a show in Saint Petersburg Russia at 11:00 pm, staying up in a band suite with everyone on the tour until the bus departure for the airport at 5:00 am. Flying from St. Pete at 7am to Moscow, holding over until noon

to fly to London. Arriving in London expecting a two hour layover that increased hour by hour into a twelve hour lay over. Finally getting into LA eleven hours later to find they had lost my luggage. Welcome home.

How to survive International Airports

1   Stay out of the bar, and away from caffeine. It'll exaggerate the effects of dehydration, and jet-lag, and weaken your immune system. You'll need as little of these complications as possible.

2   Relax, read. Take a lap top and work, or study, and alternate between that and getting up and walking around and stretching.

3   Get to know your band and crew mates. Many are actually great people despite that fact they have chosen to run away and join the circus for a living.

4   Hook your travel bag around your leg when seated. Use it as a pillow when laying down or closing your eyes. Never ask anyone to be responsible for your valuable luggage except the tour manager or an assistant.

5   Write down your flight no. and gate no. if you have a bad memory. If you have a long layover (three hours +), get a taxi and see the city. Go out for a real meal.

6   Use your free time to arrange for the best meal and seating you can get on the upcoming flight.

7   Drink lots of water.

8   Take a back pack as your carry on so you can have both hands free to browse the book stores and golf shops, sweeten your double Mocha Latte, and in general not bang into everyone in the airport with your humungous duffel bag overtime you turn around.

9   No matter what happens, don't sweat anything. Your plans may be delayed, change or fall apart. There's nothing you can do about it. Anticipate the worse, and don't be surprised when it happens.

10 Do what you can to help out. Get your own bags. Help with others bags. Stay busy, and helpful, you'll feel much better than if you sit around and bitch. I've done my fair share of both enough to know.

11 Ask the locals what the cool spots in the airport are (food, reading, sitting areas). They've been there enough to know.

12 Call someone you love and say 'Hi.' Stay connected to your roots.

Pro-file Musician: Martin Jenner

Instrument: guitar
Tours: Cliff Richard, Everly Brothers

What advice would you give anyone going on tour for the first time?

Given that, in my experience, everyone on tour reverts to childhood, two things are essential. An official disclaimer and a written apology to the parts of the body which will be the recipients of the excesses of the tour. The former reads along the lines: I, (name of disclaimer) hereby make it known that anything I may say or do for the next (length of tour) is to be totally disregarded, never referred to, and above all never held against me now, or at any future time or place. (signed by Disclaimant.) The gesture is somewhat futile of course because people do remind you of things you said and did on tour and probably will be able to provide photographic evidence as well. Still it's the thought that counts.

What are the good bits about touring?

All of it. New countries, places, the ultimate privilege of travel.

What are the bad bits?

On a personal note, missing my children grow up – an unfortunate by-product of extensive touring, and an irretrievable part of theirs and my lives.

What advice would you give musicians regarding contracts?

Get them checked. I've heard countless stories of musicians getting ripped off. It's worth making sure with a music lawyer that the contract is worth the paper it's written on, and is more watertight than the Titanic – especially if long tours and therefore large sums of money are involved.

How do you deal with living at such close quarters with fellow band members?

Our tours were both well funded and well organised so we had separate rooms and we weren't living at close quarters. However, in the early days when I started we travelled together in a tiny van to gigs. We once travelled with a keyboard player who had a different, rather quaint standard when it came to oral hygiene. His smile looked like Dresden after the RAF had hit it and he had halitosis that would knock buzzards off a shit-cart at three hundred yards. We forced him to sit in the back of the van with a big screen around him until he addressed the problem. Another musician in another band I was in in the early sixties, in the Hamburg Reeperbahn days had a unique way of selecting his stage wear for that night. He would gather a huge pile of dirty washing in his hands and hurl the whole lot into the air. He would frantically snatch at the descending apparel and whatever he caught he wore that night.

How do you amuse yourself/ stop yourself from going insane on the road?

Oh God, where does one start on this one? Among the non-arrestable wheezes are: a strategically placed coin in a light socket taking out ALL power on a hotel floor, sealing a musician into his room by running gaffer tape round the frame of the door and then calling him at 3:30 am to tell him he's wanted urgently in the foyer; altering the wiring in the back of the TV so that future guests get treated to an inverted picture; washing-up liquid in the indoor fountains would produce a novel effect etc. etc. But the two most popular pastimes involved Lifts and laundry bags.

The lifts had to be targeted as they contained irresistible magnets in the form of exquisitely shot photos. Usually at around 4:00 am someone would enter the lifts, remove the photos and after some inventive alterations they would be returned. Some while later early morning guests were treated to a smiling chef holding his culinary creation in which would be various parts of the human anatomy culled from assorted 'health' magazines, while the swimming pool photo would show bronzed, bathing beauties with Roger Whittaker's and Frank Ifield's heads superimposed. Smiling skiers would descend the local ski-slopes with large exposed breasts flying in the wind regardless of their gender.

Most hotels would remove the pictures and nothing would be said but one Hotel in Denmark took a dim view and presented us with a bill of huge proportions. That was when the word from above came that that particular method of recreation would have to cease. It did. Laundry bags were easier. Everyone collected the large bags provided by hotels for dirty laundry, and we saved them until we were in a tall hotel. The person with the highest room would be the host. The laundry bags would be filled with water and ceremoniously hurled out of the window onto the car park below. Forty odd litres of water travelling at sixty-four feet per second! It was not uncommon, while checking-out early, to view a car park decorated with mangled laundry bags. While there were many funny nights at this a couple in particular spring to mind. In Brussels a 'bombing' raid from the thirty-second floor took place with us blissfully unaware that the joint Chiefs of Staff of several countries were having a N.A.T.O. summit nearby and that the sonic results of our activities were causing much consternation among the troops guarding their hotel. Amazingly nothing was said. The final blow came when we accidentally side-swiped a rental van one night. That was another bill. After that the band and crew were never booked into rooms higher than the second floor.

What would you have in your on the road Survival Kit?
Savlon! And huge amounts of it. Musicians thrive on extremely hot curries and it is a particular quirk of nature that a Vindaloo the following morning can be likened to sitting on an oxy-acetyline torch. Also, a flight-cased, telescopic operating theatre complete with staff, donor organs, and every piece of medical equipment available to rebuild a human being.

And your road crew. Every tour or show cannot survive without a good one. It's been my long held belief that a road crew can be likened to the Swiss Army Knife of the human race in that they can take any situation and fix it, no matter what the problem. They work horrendously long hours before, during, and after the show. Quite often after the 'get out' it is necessary for them to leave immediately for the next show. It would be true to say that they are the absolute foundation of the touring side of the music business and utterly deserve the respect of both the artists and the general public alike.

What's the worst/funniest/most memorable thing that has happened to you on the road?
Far too many to relate. Worst – that's easy. Being told of my father's death and later the death of Graham Jarvis, one of my dearest and closest friends, and an awesomely talented drummer. On both occasions I was due on stage soon after receiving the news. I've often wondered if the many people who have faced the same situation, and those who may face the same scenario at some time in their career, felt, or will feel like taking an extremely heavy, blunt object and inflicting severe damage to the cretin who uttered the phrase 'the show must go on!' In retrospect though I admit that the show must, and always will go on for we've all elected to be in show business.

Have you ever experienced any memorable cultural problems touring overseas?

Trying to explain to a hotel person who didn't speak much English that, in my opinion, my previous night's mini-bar bill would, in one fell swoop, solve their national debt, was always tricky.

Also, in the Far East I discovered that it is essential to take out Life Insurance just to cross the road. Regard for human life is not in the broad scheme of things over there and even a suit of armour would be insufficient protection against the myriads of cyclists and people who race around in their 'putt-putt' motor scooters with an absolute disregard for their own and everybody else's well-being.

When the tour is over how do you adapt back to life off the road again?

When not touring I was a full-time session guitarist and allowed myself 48 hours to get over any jet-lag before piling back into the studio scene. Even though at the end of the tour everyone was tired and glad to be home to see friends and families there always was an innate sadness that it was all over, almost a sense of loss, especially after a long tour.

Fortunately for me there was little time to brood as luckily, I had a full workload to return to, but the adjustment of the 'schoolboy' mentality of a tour to the 'real' world wasn't easy.

What has been the most alarming technical problem you have experienced on stage?

In Germany in the early 60's being constantly thrown across stage by 'stray' current going through the mike to the guitar via me. The incredibly fast 'cut-out' safety devices of today were not available then. Scary moments!

Have you ever had to deal with dodgy sound systems and if so how did you deal with the problems?

Yes. If quiet and polite requests repeated more than half a dozen times failed to cure the problem the offer of a monitor suppository usually did the trick.

Pro-file Musician: Steve Howard

Instrument: trumpet, flugelhorn
Tours: Paul McCartney & Wings ('75-80), Ray Charles, Albert Collins

What advice would you give someone going on tour for the first time?

To the young musician it's probably an exciting thing to go out on the road, and at first it's a lot of fun – and a lot of people tend to think that ... well you get to go to all these really cool places and stuff like that and you do, but mainly all you see is the inside of a concert hall, a hotel, airports and such as that. You don't ... at least on my touring schedule ... usually we're doing a lot of one nighters where we will just be travelling each day, and airport, hotel concert hall, you know – soundcheck, back to the hotel. You never get to see any of the sights or anything, so it's kind of a drag. So you kind of have to prepare yourself mentally for it being a job and not just a fun trip – although there can be some fun times had it's ... it gets old after a while too, you know, when you're living out of a suitcase, extensive, long road trips ...

I know some of the guys that were on the road with Ray Charles had been on the road with Ray for six years and Ray tours nine months out of the year, and then takes off three months. Some of these guys – they only saw their wives and families for three months during the year, and then the rest of the time they were gone. And that's a tough life, it really is. It's a tough life if you spend your entire time on the road. I quite enjoyed going out, and of course working with McCartney we would go out and work for a few weeks and then we would be off 'cause he's a family man, so he didn't like to travel that much. Kind of the same thing with Albert Collins – we'd go to Europe and do a three week European tour and we'd come home and have three or four weeks off before we'd do any more jobs.

Does it take skill to live in Hotels well?

Take a book. I used to do a lot of reading when I was on the road. In my earlier days, before I got smart I used to do a lot of drinking and partying and such as that, but you can really wear yourself out ... and the food situation can be bad for you. In January I'll be forty-seven years old so when I go on the road it's hard on my body to do that, you know, eating whatever is there. Now, at home I try to eat healthy, and when you're on the road it's just next to impossible, especially if you're on the road with a group that's maybe not ... you know if you're out with a superstar or something like that you can sort of order up what you want. But when you're on the road and on a bus job

with somebody your gonna be having to eat at Denny's and places like that, and it's just not very healthy. I try to shop and carry a few things along with me whenever I can and make time, whenever possible, to get to a store and buy fruit and things like that ... just keep a little sack of something to eat.

Do you keep in touch with friends and family?
Oh yeah. Every two or three days I would call home, and then I always have an itinerary that will tell them exactly where I am if they need to reach me. Everybody does it a little different but for me, I'm more of a home kind of a guy. I don't enjoy the road ... after about the first week I'm ready to come home. Sometimes you just can't do that though – especially if you're being offered a great deal of money.

Do you spend a lot of money on phone calls?
I don't make long phone calls but we'd touch base every few days, and talk for a few minutes and it depends, if I'm in Europe I probably don't call quite as often as I would if we were in the States. And I'd try to call at a reasonable hour. I have a 1-800 number at home. If I'm in the States I can call that number and it's a cheaper rate than say, using a calling card or something like that.

You haven't run up any mega bills on tour?
I think the highest phone bill I had was for $300, and my normal phone bill is $50-$100.

Do you always have a contract when you tour or is a lot of it done on handshake agreements?
A lot of it is handshake agreement – has been in the past. When I worked with Albert Collins I didn't have a handshake agreement

with him, I'd exchange a letter or something like that but then with Paul McCartney and bigger artists there is a contract, generally speaking. Because, the more the money is the more everybody wants to be secure.

What sort of things do you think are important to have in a contract?

When you're working for Ray Charles or somebody like that the job pays what it pays, and that's it. So there's no need for a contract or anything like that – you might have some sort of an agreement that you might sign with them. And the Musicians Union dictates also that, for instance, if you're playing the job live and they want to, say, record the thing, well, you're supposed to get paid extra for that – if they do a live recording. A lot of times artists will try to not pay you for that – I don't think it's necessarily the artists as much as it is their management. It's a very important thing to get a music attorney, so that you can be covered on all sorts of things like that, so that if they decide to make a film of part of a concert, or press a record, or do a television show, or take a little clip of you playing to make a Pepsi commercial, or whatever – that you can be compensated for that.

How do you decide what to take on tour with you?

I'm a trumpet player so I don't have as much stuff to carry around, just my trumpet and my flugel horn and such as that, but I'd try to figure out what the climate is of the place that I'm going to. For instance, say if you're going to Australia their summers are our winters, so you have to be aware of where you're going and what the weather's like as far as packing your correct wardrobe and stuff like that. I'm not as good at it as some. We had a drummer on the road with us, he was a real road rat, and he had one small suitcase and he never smelled bad or anything so I know he was keeping his clothes clean, and stuff like that but he didn't have a lot of stuff to have to carry around. 'Cause if you carry a big huge suitcase and horns and a carry-on bag and all that stuff and dragging it through an airport every day it can get really, really tiring to carry all that around. So I try to travel as light as possible. If you look at your itinerary you can see where you're gonna be – know when you're gonna be in a place maybe for two days – okay, there's a good opportunity to get some laundry done. You can sort of plan it out that way – look at your itinerary and see what your longest run's gonna be, and pack that many pairs of socks.

QUOTE

Look at your itinerary and see what your longest run's gonna be, and pack that many pairs of socks.

Musicians are renowned for practical joking, have you experienced that first hand?

We always try to have a lot of fun – there's a lot of cutting up and a lot of joking, like that but as far as really pulling a stunt ... sometimes on stage, I try to wait until somebody, like the saxophone player is playing a solo or something like that I'll say something funny or make a comment about something that'll mess him up a little bit.

I know John Smith, my partner in The White Trash Horns, he's always concerned about his hair looking right. I'm kind of about half bald anyway so it doesn't really bother me and I'm always like ... and he'll say 'Is my moustache straight?,' and I'll say 'Oh, yeah.' So one night he's getting ready to play and I kept kind of looking at him and he was just getting ready to play this solo and he said 'What are you looking at?,' and I said 'Oh man, your moustache is all crooked, it's all messed up,' and he kind of like flipped out. Then of course he had to play, and the spotlight was gonna be on him and all that, and it wasn't, it wasn't messed up at all but I just kind of threw him into a little trick back there. He's my partner and I've been working with him for a long time, and we're always goofing around with each other in little ways like that.

Do you ever have problems with gear getting damaged?

No, because I carry my instruments with me. But I can guarantee you, if you check a horn on, even in a hard case – horns are such delicate instruments – especially saxophones. Check one on and it's gonna get messed up some kind of way because the airline people they just look at it as a piece of luggage, and they're just tossing it about, and it's really pretty dicey to be putting your horns in the luggage. Now some guys have anvil cases built that their horn case will actually fit into, you know, those padded steel cases. If you had a lot of instruments or say it was a baritone saxophone and you couldn't check it on the plane ... but I have a trumpet case. It's made by a company called Reunion Blues. It's an instrument bag company, they make bags for guitars and saxophones and trumpets and everything – it's from San Francisco. A lot of the guys use these now and it's made ... my bag will hold a trumpet and a Flugel horn, plus I've got room for my mutes in there. It's a padded bag and it meets the requirements for size for a carry-on bag for the airlines so I can just take it anywhere I need to go with me.

Pro-file Musician: Susie Davis

Instrument: keyboards
Tours: Billy Idol, Sinead O'Connor, Van Morrison

What is the first thing you do when you get the phone call inviting you to join a tour?

You brace yourself, take a deep breath and get ready to descend into madness. In a short period of time you'll be immersed into a whole new social scene and all the subtle group dynamics that go along with it. You'll be leaving your home life and entering into an intense relationship with a new temporary family of people. You'll experience exhilaration, ego gratification, boredom, and loneliness. At the end of it you'll step off the tour bus, wave goodbye to your comrades, most of whom you may only see rarely if at all now that the tours over, and return to your old life, feeling like Dorothy returning to Kansas after her sojourn in Oz.

How do you decide what gear to take?

Each tour dictates what gear you'll need. Artists usually hand you CD's or tapes of the songs they need you to learn and you begin by trying to duplicate the parts and sounds on the records. You may need to sample sounds, or write sequences, and for sure if you're a keyboardist you'll need to do a lot of programming, so it all depends. Be prepared for long work days though. A twelve hour work day is often the norm when putting a tour together unless your lucky and all you have to do is play Hammond Organ or Piano.

Any advice that you would give to someone going out on tour for the first time?

Beware of excess partying. Your social life will center around the people in your entourage, who in many cases are people that you would normally never hang out with. The one ritual that binds a bunch of disparate personality types together is social drinking and it's real easy to find yourself drinking often for this reason. I find that too much alcohol over an extended period of time brings on bouts of insomnia and depression. It's important to keep your spirits up and stay in good health so try and be moderate with alcohol intake.

Susie – up close and
personal with Mick Jagger

Is there anything you wish you had known in advance before starting a career in music?

I wish that I had foreseen the unpredictabilityof touring; the ups
and downs that occur in salary and in the availability of work.
When you're in the middle of a stretch of work, its easy to
believe that your good fortune will go on forever, that touring
work will be plentiful, and that the money will always be good,
but this is far from reality. Even though I did a tour with a
known artist almost every year for about a thirteen year stretch,
sometimes these tours would only be six to eight weeks long,
leaving me with ten months out of the year to find other ways
to make money. I also didn't foresee my getting bored with the
lifestyle of touring, and when I did and started looking around
for other ways of making a living, I found myself with a real
lack of marketable skills to rely upon. My advice to young
players is to pursue your dreams, but don't loose sight of the
future. Be aware that someday, you will either be tired of
touring or the work will dry up, and you may need to do
something else to make a living. I feel like a Mom when I say
this, but try to give yourself something to fall back on. Get your
college degree, study computer arts, journalism, or whatever it is
that interests you. Unfortunately talent gives no guarantee of
success especially in the music business, so plan ahead.

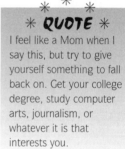

✳ **QUOTE** ✳
I feel like a Mom when I
say this, but try to give
yourself something to fall
back on. Get your college
degree, study computer
arts, journalism, or
whatever it is that
interests you.

Susie touring with Billy Idol in the 70s

What are the good bits about touring?

The vibe on the tour bus is often one of a mobile summer camp. Your life at home has been left behind and with it, many of the responsibilities that go with it. Your only responsibility is to stay healthy, make your lobby calls on time and play well during the concerts. Most decisions are made for you, like where and when you have to be someplace, and even meals are largely taken care of (and can be well prepared if your lucky and get good catering). Depending on the pace of the tour there is often a lot of time to kill and many opportunities to pursue relaxing activities like rollerblading, working out, watching TV, reading, being a tourist, taking long baths etc., (things that I often have trouble finding time for when I'm at home). If your lucky and get on a major tour with real live rock stars, all the hubbub and VIP treatment can be quite fun. Strangers want to meet you, get your autograph, be your friend. The ego is gratified in many ways on tour.

No performer no matter how jaded can be wholly immune to the enthusiasm of a live audience. There is also a satisfying feeling of 'going someplace' with your life that I think comes largely from the fact that you're on a bus every night and you are going someplace. It's no place really, just another hotel, another backstage, another airport, but the constant traveling feeds that illusion.

Getting the opportunity to visit other countries and experience their cultures is probably the greatest benefit of getting to tour. I've had some wonderful adventures in many countries of the world, and I was being paid the whole time.

Exposure to different types of people is a wonderful benefit as well. On a tour with a French pop chanteuse, the most diverse group of people I ever traveled with was assembled and we became a traveling 'little village' of diverging ethnicities, cultures, sexes, ages, and sexual persuasions. French, Mexican, African, American, Female, Male, Gay, Straight, people in their 20's through their 40's, it turned out to be one of the most fun groups I had ever toured with. Music does bring us the gift of being a common language that connects us to people we would otherwise have nothing in common with.

It's really the people you are working with that will make a tour a success or a failure. When you hook up with a great group it can be non-stop craziness and immensely entertaining. The music I played had little to do with the tours I have the most fond memories of, because in the end, you're only on stage for an hour and a half tops five or six times a week. In comparison you spend hours together every day with your group of fellow travelers. When it's good, it's very good, and when it's bad its ...

What are the bad bits?

Staying healthy can be a real challenge. Getting enough quality sleep can be a problem if your the kind of person who has trouble sleeping on a tour bus. Also, most nights you'll leave the gig, get on the bus and arrive at your destination at four or five in the morning. If you're lucky you've gotten a couple hours sleep but then you have to wake up, gather up your belongings and move into your room and try to fall back asleep again. It's tempting to take medication to make sure you sleep enough, but I've found that those kinds of drugs often leave you with a hangover and can lead to moods of depression.

The quality of the relationship that you have with the other members of your touring entourage has everything to do with how much fun a tour ends up being. So sometimes its great and other times it 'aint. So much of the time on the road you are surrounded by people yet if there is no one you feel you can really relate to, you can feel like the loneliest person in the world.

If you've taken a tour with an artist and you don't really like the music, things can get pretty bleak a month or so into the tour. Endless travel, shallow friendships, the feeling of having no life of your own can really start to get to you without the joy that comes with performing music that you love.

Often a band may only get to play for 45 minutes, 5 to 6 nights a week. That's not very much music making for the amount of time you spend on the bus, in the hotel room, and backstage at the venue. Often the hotels you stay at are located in Industrial Parks miles outside of the nearest city and there is literally nothing to do on a day off except take a cab to the local mall. I brought Rollerblades with me on tour because I got tired of opening up my curtains in the morning, and seeing that our hotel was in the middle of a sea of concrete next to a freeway somewhere, and feeling trapped. This way I could at least get the illusion of having some freedom.

That's the price you pay. Although it can be lovely having most of your responsibilities taken out of your hands, being told where to go and when to be there, and leading a generally carefree life, you sacrifice you own life to get that. It's easy to feel trapped then because you have little opportunity to make decisions for yourself and your life is definitely not your own.

Besides your gear what personal stuff do you take on the road for entertainment or its comfort value?

I'm an activity based person and so I carry around much more stuff on the road than I ever use. What's important to me is to have lots of entertainment options and so I bring lots of books to read, music to study, art supplies, Roller Blades, music CDs, Ghetto Blaster, vocalizing tapes, camera, journal. On some tours I've brought out a porta studio so that I could write and record in my hotel room. I never know what I'm going to feel like doing at any given moment so I want to give myself lots of options, but this means that I'm always carting around shoulder bags filled with toys that weigh a ton. I'm always jealous of the people who have one small bag and don't seem to need to lug around a ton of stuff with them all the time. One time I was carrying so much stuff with me as I climbed out of the bus that I simply lost balance and fell on my butt, slightly twisting an ankle in the process.

To make synthetic filled hotel rooms a bit more hospitable I've carried around a Humidifier (Hotel rooms can be notoriously dry) Incense, Big Scarfs to drape over glaring hotel lamps, (make sure they're not going to get hot and catch on fire!), and a citrus spray you get at health food stores that when sprayed in a room, not only smells nice, but attaches itself to synthetic particles and negative ions and helps to eliminate them from the stuffy room air.

What advice would you give female musician's about life on the road?

In general, finding yourself in so many different situations with so many different people requires any one to be a good diplomat and a bit of a chameleon. Anybody in a touring band has to be delicate in how they offer suggestions and deal with other musicians fragile egos. You need to sense what is appropriate behavior and be able to fit your own personality in their somewhere. As a woman in a largely male environment, sometimes you can really feel like the odd person out. Women are usually treated just like one of the guys in the band, (no special treatment in other words) but are often not considered one of the guys enough to be included in their social plans and can end up feeling a bit left out. I learned how to compensate for that by just becoming super independent. I love to explore new cities and often just hit the pavement to see what's around me as soon as I hit a new town. I've had wonderful adventures all around the world because I took the initiative to go exploring on my own. If we were in a foreign country, I would often extend my stay past when the rest of the band returned home and play super tourist for a week or so.

My advice is to just be cautious about entering into romantic liaisons with members of the touring entourage. Women in general can tend to imbue a sexual relationship with more emotional meaning than a man might, and if a man breaks things off or behaves in a disrespectful way it can be devastating, especially because the touring environment can be very lonely, even with all those people around. A tour should be a fun and adventurous time and your main responsibility is to stay healthy, play well and keep a good attitude. Remember that it's hard on everybody and the more supportive you are of each other the better time everyone will have. I've seen too many woman, upset over a road relationship gone sour, let it ruin the overall experience for them. I'm just saying to be wary, because the wrong decision can change your overall perception of a tour, and you deserve to have as good a time as you possibly can.

One woman I worked with had a romance with a musician from another band on the tour, got pregnant, got dumped, and then had to get an abortion and her resulting grief and depression over the whole thing effected everybody down to the bus drivers. So women be wise...

✳ QUOTE ✳
My advice is to just be cautious about entering into romantic liaisons with members of the touring entourage. Women in general can tend to imbue a sexual relationship with more emotional meaning than a man might, and if a man breaks things off or behaves in a disrespectful way it can be devastating.

Pro-file Musician: Tim Scott

Instrument: bass
Tours: Tower of Power, Stevie Wonder

How do you cope with sharing rooms with band members?

Well, that's a real tough one. I try not to do that anymore. I don't really have to as a rule. The best thing is to pick out the person that you like the most, that you think you're gonna get along with the best. If you get stuck with someone you don't like you'd better buy yourself some handcuffs. There's usually a kind of natural pairing off system, where people gravitate towards each other.

Do things ever get to blows?

I've seen it a couple of times, I've never been engaged in any of that. You need a lot of patience and tolerance and acceptance of peoples behaviour of their habits.

What are the good bits of touring?

For me, I still enjoy travelling. I know people that get burned out on it but I just like seeing other places – I like going to other towns. With your schedule though you're usually just in and out so if you want to see a town you've got to have a plan about how much time you've got and what you want to see. Take cabs and go to places of interest.

What are the bad bits?

For one thing, it's really hard on one's health. The wear and tear … you usually don't eat as well as one should on the road, so nutritionally speaking it can be a bad deal. Like for me in particular I have back problems. When I fly I'm always in a cramped seat for long hours and it's real hard on me, and I'm packing an instrument – my bass, I carry it in a bag on my back, and it sets my back out of alignment if I'm walking across an airport for long distances with that. So I always come back just a little beat up from the experience. That and not getting enough sleep, with timetables and stuff; jet-lag; losing hours.

Do you work out on the road?

I have a stretching programme that I do for my back – but aside from that there's usually not time to go to a gym or anything like that.

How do you cope with living in hotels?
I don't mind it. I really don't mind it 'cos I don't have to make
the bed ... I don't have to clean up. And I don't live like a pig in
hotels either, 'cos I don't like to but it's pretty cool that you
don't have to clean up.

What is you phone habit like?
I use a calling card. I use a calling card and charge all my long
distance calls to my home phone. All you pay is ... some hotels
don't charge a surcharge still but if they do it's fairly nominal ...
and so I just get the one bill at my house.

What's the most expensive single phone call you've had?
$300. I have a girlfriend in Seattle right now so my phone bills
are awful.

What do you take with you on tour?
I travel really lightly. On the bigger tours people take all kinds of
stuff, and actually some of the guys in my band will take golf
clubs with them. We're going to Park City Utah for the World
Cup Skiing and everybody in the band ... I think everybody but
me skis, so they'll have their ski gear with them, but for me I
like to travel really light. Sometimes I'll take ... I think music's
really important. You'll be on the road and most everybody has
a portable cassette or CD Player with headphones that they can
use on the plane and in their room. And I'll take some books.

**What's the worst thing that's happened to you on the
road? You had an unusual experience at the Atlanta
Olympics.**
Yeah, I would say that that one gig was probably the best and
worst experience that I've ever had as a musician. Being that it
was the Olympics, it was really an exciting and joyful time for
the band because we were entertaining the world, basically.
People from all over the world were coming and we were playing
for audiences of fifteen to twenty thousand a night, and it just
felt like it could have gone on forever. We were playing on the
AT&T stage in the Centennial Park and every night there would
be a headliner like Santana or Joan Osborne, Little Feat, and then
they would shut down the stage and do the nightly news, NBC
news feed for a recap of the days Olympic events and then we
would come on and do a party after that and we had some huge
crowds. It was the biggest sound system, biggest stage that
we've ever played on. There was a room underneath us ... this

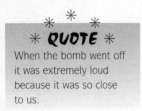

was an incredible stage and there was just racks and racks and
racks of amplifiers – I've never seen so many. The stage was
built over soundproof booths, for all the NBC affiliates. Each one
had a booth and that's where they did their broadcast. When the
bomb went off it was extremely loud because it was so close to
us – it was like a hundred and fifty feet from the stage. It was
the sound tower, there were two towers out in front of the
stage, and one of them they were running lights from and the
other they were running sound from. And it was the sound
tower that blew up. And it was incredibly loud because the
sound fed-back through the PA system and came right at us
through the monitors. Actually my ears rang for about two
weeks after that, and I felt the concussion – it kind of knocked
me back a little bit and thumped in my chest, and it blew debris
up on stage. The tower was covered with corrugated metal and it
through bits of corrugated metal up there.

Was anybody on stage hurt?
No, the drummer had his arm brushed by some stuff, the FBI
pulled out some – it was a pipe bomb with nails and screws in it,
they dug some of that stuff out of the stage. We were extremely
lucky. It was just the trajectory of it that it didn't get us.

Something like that would take a while to get over.
Yeah. It happened and some of us knew exactly what it was. I
looked up and saw smoke, that's all I saw and I saw some people
running and a stagehand came up and said 'okay, we've gotta
get you off the stage right now.' And they just rushed us off the
stage and out the back, and it was pandemonium out on the
street. All the news crews that were leaving for the night were
running back towards the Centennial Park ... and our producer
who was with us was actually out at the tower, and he was
helping some people doing triage when the emergency crews got
there. And so we were walking to the van and some policeman
heard that he had been there and witnessed the whole thing, and
grabbed him and took him off to be interviewed by the FBI.

Did you play there again after that?
That was the end of our gig. I actually played there the next
week with another band from Los Angeles. But they decided not
to have any more night events so we played during the day.

Have you ever experienced any cultural problems over seas?
Other than not speaking a particular language, no, I haven't.

What's been the most alarming technical problem you've ever had on stage?
This didn't involve my equipment but ... originally I'm from Seattle and I had a band up there and we used to back up a lot of national artists, and we got to play with the late Big Joe Turner, the Blues singer, and ... but this was right toward the end of his life and he had some real serious physical problems. He had diabetes and he had circulation problems in both legs, a heart condition ... and so he didn't stand on stage he would sit. He walked with two crutches and he just had a microphone right there in front of him. And so we played this set for him, in this little club, and when the show was over we would play what they call a 'chaser' which is just background music that we vamp on while the artist would walk off the stage. So he went to get out of that chair and um ... his legs buckled under him and he fell back into the drum set and completely wiped it out ... and we're all trying to play ... it was one of the more embarrassing moments in my life – I felt very bad for him. He passed away about a year later.

When the tour is over how easy is it to adapt back to life off the road again?
It's really a problem. I don't know what it's like in other cities but in Los Angeles if you're not around people forget about you – except for your friends. I've noticed that people go out on the road and if you're out for any length of time and you don't stay in contact with people, when you get back it's extremely hard to plug back in and work. Most people keep checking their messages all the time and try to book gigs for when they get back – just to keep things moving smoothly.

How come you get to play with so many diverse artists?
Well, for me, I love all different kinds of music, and I love the challenge of playing different kinds of music. And I've also found it's really helpful for trying to stay working, and stay busy. The more versatile I can become then the more sought after I am.

You played with Eric Clapton once.
I played with him once, yeah. I was doing a gig with Dr. John and Eric was there and we got him to come up and sit in. And that was a wonderful gig – it took me a week to come down from that one. I got to stand right next to him ... he was just great. I asked him ... I said, 'Do you wanna sing something?' and he said ' well, I don't know what I'd sing,' and I'm thinking – well I don't know, maybe one of your millions of hits, anything. But you know how he is, he just wants to stand at the back and noodle.

Chaka Khan was in that list as well.
She's great. She's like one of the guys. She's been in the business for so long and she's used to being in bands that are almost all guys. She really comes in and takes charge. She knows what she wants, and she's great ... she's great fun.

Musicians are often renowned for being practical jokers as well, has that been your experience on tours?
I've had a few jokes played on me. It usually involves ruining the bed that you plan on sleeping in. Someone poured beer into my bed once. It was soggy and it smelled bad. I've also had some shaving cream put in my bed and I' actually had someone take some cheese and jam it into the lock on my hotel room door and so I couldn't get in.

What advice would you give to people regarding drugs and alcohol?
It's an area that I'm pretty well versed in. I've been in recovery for over four years now.

It's really hard to say. Because I'm a member of a twelve step group I do a lot of speaking to people about that and especially to adolescents. And it's really hard to tell kids, you know, don't do this. At that age I know that I wouldn't listen to anybody about it. 'Cos I was just getting started, and I had to do about twenty-five years of research before I found out that it didn't work for me. I guess the only advice I could say is 'be careful.' Don't let it get out of hand.

Is it easier for it to get out of hand when you are on tour?
Towards the end of my using I acquired a nasty habit, and when you're out on the road it's very difficult to acquire and stay well. It was a problem for me on many occasions. So you just end up being sick – and it really detracts from the whole experience. You want to be conscious, do the job and enjoy yourself.

What happened for me was my band did what's called an 'intervention' with me and they said that I was out of control and they were concerned about me, and they wanted me to get some help. They had this guy named Buddy Arnold – Buddy Arnold is the Head of the Musicians Assistance Program and he came and facilitated the intervention and got me into a treatment. What MAP does is they get funds from the record companies to support drug rehabilitation programs for musicians because most musicians – by the time they get to the point where they need help, they can't afford it – because there's no health insurance for us. We get nothing to fall back on, so this group probably saved my life, and I know that they have for a whole bunch of my friends, people that I know. And so it's very worth mentioning that if there's anybody out there in music and they're having a tough time and they don't know what to do, they should call them.

Were you resistant to getting that help at the time or were you ready for it?
I was ready. I was really beat up and I was ready, I just didn't know what to do or where to turn.

How did the organisation help?
They have a couple of facilities out in the desert that they refer people to and they provide as much funding as they can for it. In my case they did a co pay with Riverside County, and sent me out to the desert. And it was the best thing that I ever did for myself. And afterwards they've got a private aftercare program where they have sober living facilities you can go to if you're not quite ready to come home, or go wherever you're gonna go, or if you've lost everything and you have nowhere to go, you can go there. And they have an encounter kind of therapy group twice a week. They work out of the musicians union. They have some licensed therapists that facilitate these groups, and they hold benefits around town they've had some at House of Blues and Billboard Live, with people like Bonnie Raitt and Natalie Cole performing and it's a really great organisation. I'm very grateful to them.

* **QUOTE** *
This group probably saved my life, and I know that they have for a whole bunch of my friends, people that I know. And so it's very worth mentioning that if there's anybody out there in music and they're having a tough time and they don't know what to do, they should call them.

14
Useful addresses

Korg

Korg USA Inc.
316 South Service Road
Melville
NY 11747
Tel: 516-333-9100
Fax: 516-333-9108

Korg Inc. Japan
11-17 Shimotakaido
1 Chome
Suginami-Ku
Tokyo 168

Korg UK
9 Newmarket Court
Kingston
Milton Keynes
MK10 0AU
Tel: 01908-857100
Fax: 01908-85719

Roland

North and South America
Argentina
Instumentos Musicales S.A.

Florida 638
(10050) Buenos Aires, Argentina
Tel: 01-394-4029

Brazil
Roland Brasil Ltda.
R. Coronel Octaviano da Silveira
203
05522-010 Sao Paulo, Brazil
Tel: 011-843-9377

Canada
Roland Canada Music Ltd. (Head
Office)
5480 Parkwood Way
Richmond B.C., V6V 2M4
Canada
Tel: 0604-270-6626

Roland Canada Music Ltd.
(Toronto Office)
Unit 2, 109 Woodbine Downs
Blvd.,
Etobicoke, ON M9W 6W1
Canada
Tel: 0416-213-9707

Mexico
Casa Veerkamp, s.a. de c.v.
Av. Toluca No. 323
Col. Olivar de los Padres
01780 Mexico D.F.,
Mexico
Tel: 525-668-0480

La Casa Wagner de Guadalajara
s.a. de c.v.
Av. Corona No. 202 S.J.
Guadalajara, Jalisco,
Mexico
Tel: 03-613-1414

Panama
Productos Superiores, S.A.
Apartado 655 - Panama 1
Republic De Panama
Tel: 263322

USA
Roland Corporation U.S.
7200 Dominion Circle
Los Angeles,
CA 90040-3696
U.S.A.
Tel: 213-685-5141

Venezuela
Musicland Digital C.A.
Av. Francisco de Miranda
Centro Parque de Cristal
Nivel C2 Local 20
Caracas, Venezuela
Tel: 02-285-9218

Australia and NZ
Australia
Roland Corporation Australia
Pty. Ltd.
38 Campbell Avenue
Dee Why West, NSW 2099
Australia
Tel: 2-982-8266

New Zealand
Roland Corporation (NZ) Ltd.
97 Mt. Eden Road
Mt. Eden
Auckland 3
New Zealand
Tel: 9-3098-715

Asia
China
Beijing Xinghai Musical
Instruments Co., Ltd.
2 Huangmuchang Chao Yang

District
Beijing, China
Tel: 010-6774-7491

Hong Kong
Tom Lee Music Co., Ltd. Service
Division
22-32 Pun Shan Street
Tsuen Wan
New Territories
Hong Kong
Tel: 2415-0911

Indonesia
PT Galestra Inti
Kompleks Perkantoran
Duta Merlin Blok E No. 6-7
Jl. Gajah Mada No. 3-5
Jakarta 10130
Indonesia
Tel: 021-6335416

Korea
Cosmos Corporation Service
Station
261 2nd Floor Nak-Won
Arcade
Jong-Ro ku
Seoul, Korea
Tel: 02-742-8844

Malaysia
Bentley Music SDN BHD
No. 142, Jalan Bukit Bintang
55100
Kuala Lumpur, Malaysia
Tel: 03-2443333

Philippines
G.A. Yupangco & Co. Inc.,
339 Gil J. Puyat Avenue
Makati
Metro Manila 1200
Philippines
Tel: 02-899-9801

Singapore
Swee Lee Company
Block 231, Bain Street #03-23
Bras Basah Complex
Singapore 0718
Tel: 336-7886

Cristofori Music Pte Ltd.,
335, Joo Chiat Road
Singapore 1542
Tel: 345-0435

Taiwan
Siruba Enterprise (Taiwan) Co.,
Ltd.,
Room 5, 9 fl. No. 112 Chung
Shan
N. Road Sec. 2
Taipei, Taiwan, R.O.C.
Tel: 02-561-3339

Thailand
Theera Music Co., Ltd.,
330 Verng Nakorn Kasem, Soi
2
Bangkok 10100
Thailand
Tel: 02-224-8821

Middle East
Bahrain
Moon Stores
Bad Al Bahrain Road
P.O. Box 20077
State of Bahrain
Tel: 211005

Iran
Taradis
Mir Emad Ave, No. 15, 10th
Street
P.O. Box 15875
4171 Teheran, Iran
Tel: 021-875-6524

Israel
Halilit P. Greenspoon & Sons
Ltd.,
8 Retzif Ha'aliya Hashnya St.
Tel-Aviv-Yafo
Israel
Tel: 03-682-3666

Jordan
Amman Trading Agency
Prince Mohammed Street
P.O. Box 825
Amman 11118 Jordan
Tel: 06-641200

Kuwait
Easa Husain Al Yousifi
P.O. Box 126 Safat
13002 Kuwait
Tel: 571-9499

Lebanon
A. Chahine & Fils
PO Box 16-5857 Gergi Zeidan
St.

Chahine Building, Achrafieh
Beirut, Lebanon
Tel: 01-335799

Oman
OHI Electronics and Trading
Co., LLC
P.O. Box 889
Muscat
Sultanate of Oman
Tel: 706010

Qatar
Badie Studio & Stores
P.O. Box 62, Doha, Qatar
Tel: 423554

Saudi Arabia
Abdul Latif S. Al-Ghamdi
Trading Establishment
Middle East Commercial Centre
Al-Khobar Dharan Highway
W/hamood St.
P.O. Box 3631 Al-Khober
31952 Saudi Arabia
Tel: 03-898-2332

Syria
Technical Light and Sound
Centre
Khaled Ebn Al Walid St.
P.O. Box 13520
Damascus, Syria
Tel: 011-2235-384

Turkey
Barkat Sanayi ve Ticaret
Siraselvia Cad. Guney Ishani
No.
86/6 Taksim
Istanbul, Turkey
Tel: 0212-2499324

U.A.E.
Zak Electronics & Musical
Instruments Co.,
Zabeel Road, Al Sherooq
Building
No. 14, Grand Floor
P.O. Box 8050
Dubai, U.A.E.
Tel: 04-360715

Egypt
Al Fanny Trading Office
9, Ebn Hagar Ai Askalany
Street
Ard El Golf, Heliopolis

Cairo, Egypt
Tel: 02-4171828

Africa
Kenya
Musik Land Ltd.,
P.O. Box 12183 Moi Avenue
Nairobi
Republic of Kenya
Tel: 2-338-346

Mauritius
Philanne Music Center
4th Floor Noll, Happy World
House
Sir William Newton Street
Port Luis, Mauritious
Tel: 242-2986

Reunion
FO-YAM Marcel
25 Rue Jules Merman ZL
Chaudron - BP79 97491
Ste Clotilde, Reunion
Tel: 282916

South Africa
That Other Music Shop PTY
Ltd.,
11 Melle Street (cnr Melle and
Juta Street)
Braamfontein 2001
Republic of South Africa
Tel: 011-403-4105

Paul Bothner (PTY) Ltd.,
17 Wermuller Centre
Claremont 7700
Republic of South Africa
Tel: 021-64-4030

Europe
Austria
E. Dematte & Co.
Neu-Rum Siemens-Strasse 4
P.O. Box 83
A-6040 Innsbruck, Austria
Tel: 0512-26 44 260

Belgium / Holland /
Luxembourg
Roland Benelux N.V.
Houtstraat 1 B-2260
Oevel-Westerlo, Belgium
Tel: 014-575811

Belorussia
Tushe
UL. Rabkorovskaya 17

220001 Minsk
Tel: 0172-764-911

Cyprus
Radex Sound Equipment Ltd.,
17 Diagorou St. P.O. Box 2046
Nicosia, Cyprus
Tel: 02-453-426

Denmark
Roland Scandinavia A/S
Langebrogade 6 Post Box 1937
DK-1023 Copenhagen K,
Denmark
Tel: 32 95 3111

France
Musikengro
Zac de Folliouses 01706
Les Eschets, Miribel, France
Tel: 472 26 2700

Finland
Roland Scandinavia As, Filial
Finland
Lauttasaarentie 54B
Fin-00201, Helsinki, Finland
P.O. Box 109
Tel: 0-682-4020

Germany
Roland Elektronische
Musikinstrumente
Handelsgesellschaft mbH
Oststrasse 96, 22844
Norderstedt, Germany
Tel: 040-52-60090

Greece
V. Dimitriadis & Co. Ltd.,
20 Alexandras St. &
Bouboulinas 54 St.
106 82 Athens, Greece
Tel: 01-8232415

Hungary
Intermusica Ltd.,
Warehouse Area 'DEPO' Pf.83
H-2046 Torokbalint, Hungary
Tel: 23-338-041

Ireland
The Dublin Service Centre
Audio Maintenance Limited
11 Brunswick Place
Dublin 2
Republic of Ireland
Tel: 01-677322

Italy
Roland Italy S.p.A.
Viale delle Industrie, 8
20020 Arese, Milano, Italy
Tel: 02-93581311

Norway
Roland Scandinavia Avd.
Kontor Norge
Lilleakerveien 2 Postboks 95
Lilleaker N-0216 Oslo, Norway
Tel: 273-0074

Poland
P.P.H. Brzostowicz Marian
UL Blokowa 32
03624 Warszawa, Poland
Tel: 022-679-44-19

Portugal
Caius-Tecnologias Audio e
Musica, Lda.
Rue de Catarina 131
4000 Porto, Portugal
Tel: 02-38-4456

Russia
Petroshop Ltd.,
11 Sayanskaya Street
Moscow, 11531, Russia
Tel: 095-307-4892

Slami Music Company
Sadojava-Triumfalnaja St., 16
103006, Moscow, Russia
Tel: 095-209-2193

Spain
Roland Electronics de Espana
S.A.
Calle Bolivia 239
08020 Barcelona, Spain
Tel: 93-308-1000

Sweden
Roland Scandinavia A/S
Danvik Center 28 A, 2tr.
S-131 30 Nacka, Sweden
Tel: 08-702-0020

Switzerland
Roland (Switzerland) AG
Musitronic AG
Gerberstrasse 5
CH-4410 Liestal, Switzerland
Tel: 061-921-1615

Ukraine
TIC-TAC
Mira Str. 19/108
P.O. Box 180
295400 Munkachevo, Ukraine
Tel: 03131-414-40

United Kingdom
Roland U.K. Ltd.,
Swansea Office
Atlantic Close, Swansea
Enterprise Park, Swansea
West Glamorgan SA7 9FJ
United Kingdom
Tel: 01792-702701

Yamaha

Yamaha Europe
UK
Yamaha UK Ltd.
Sherbourne Drive
Tilbrook, Milton Keynes
MK7 8BL

Yamaha R&D Centre London
Yamaha MusicSoft Europe Ltd.
Unit 6, The Piazza
3 Devonhurst Place
Chiswick, London W4 4JE

Yamaha Electronics UK Ltd.
Yamaha House
200 Rickmansworth Road
Watford, Herts. WD1 7JS

Germany
Yamaha Europa G.m.b.H/
Yamaha Elektronik Europa
G.m.b.H/
Yamaha Systems Technology
Europe
Siemensstr. 22-34, D-25462
Rellingen. b.
Hamburg, Germany

Yamaha Atelier fur
Blasinstrumente
Freiherr-vom-Stein-Str. 20R,
D-63263
Neu-Isenburg, Germany

France
Yamaha Musique France S.A./
Yamaha Electronique France
S.A.
Parc d'Activites de Paris-Est
Rue Ambroise Croizat

77183 Croissy-Beaubourg

Centre Europeen des Activites
Artistiques Pianos Yamaha
17, Rue Dumont-d'Urville
75116 Paris
France

Yamaha Electronique Alsace
S.A.
Rue de Martelberg B.P.9,
Monswiller 67700
Saverne, France

Italy
Yamaha Musica Italia s.p.a.
Viale Italia 88,
20020 Lainate (Milano)
Italia

Spain
Yamaha-Hazen Electronica
Musical S.A.
Jorge Juan 30
28001 Madrid, Spain

Scandinavia
Yamaha Scandinavia A.B.
J A Wettergrens gata 1,
Vastra Flolunda, Sweden

Yamaha Asia
Japan
Yamaha Corporation
10-1, Nakazawa-cho
Hamamatsu, Shizuoka Pref.,
430, Japan

China
Tianjin Yamaha Electronic
Musical Instruments, Inc.
N. 130 Dongting Road, TEDA,
Tianjin
People's Republic of China

Guangzhou Yamaha-Pearl
River Piano Inc.
Jing 2 Road, 3 Heng Road
East Zone
GETDD, Guangzhou
People's Republic of China

Yamaha Trading (Shanghai)
Co., Ltd.
Room 728 Shanghai Centre
1376 Nanjing Road (W),
Shanghai
People's Republic of China

Xiaoshan Yamaha Musical Instrument Co., Ltd.
No. 2 South Jianshe Road Xiaoshan Economic and Technical Development Zone, Zhejiang, People's Republic of China

Hong Kong
Yamaha Electronics (China)
Room 2507, 25/F, Lippo Tower Lippo Centre, 89 Queensway, Hong Kong

Taiwan
Taiwan Yamaha Musical Instrument Mfg. Co., Ltd.
10th Floor, Yeong-Hsin Bldg., No. 6 Nanking E. Rd., Sec. 2 Taipei, Taiwan

Yamaha KHS Music Co., Ltd.
10F, 150, Tun-Hwa North Road
Taipei, Taiwan

Kaohsiung Yamaha Co., Ltd.
Zhong Yang Road, Nantze Export Processing Zone Kaohsiung, Taiwan

SE Asia
P.T. Yamaha Music Indonesia Jalan Jend Gatot Subroto Kav. 4
Jakarta 12930, Indonesia

P.T. Yamaha Indonesia
Jalan Rawagelam 1-5, Kawasan Industri
Pulogadung, Jakarta Timur Indonesia

P.T. Yamaha Music Manufacturing Indonesia
JL. Pulobuaran Raya No. 1, Kawasan Industri
Pulogadung, Jakarta Timur Indonesia

P.T. Yamaha Musical Products Indonesia
JL. Rembang Industri 1/36 Kawasan Industri Pier, Pasuruan, Java Timur Indonesia

P.T. Yamaha Music Manufacturing Asia
MM2100 Industrial Town, EE-3
Cibitung, Bekas: 17520, West Java, Indonesia

Yamaha Music (Asia) Pte. Ltd.
80, Tannery Lane,
Singapore 1334, Singapore

Yamaha Systems Technology Singapore Pte. Ltd.
138 Cecil Street, #03-01A, Cecil Court
Singapore, 069538
Singapore

Yamaha Electronics Asia Pte. Ltd.
138 Cecil Street, #05-02/03, Cecil Court
Singapore, 069538, Singapore

Siam Music Yamaha Co., Ltd.
RS Tower 17th Floor, 121/60-61 Rachadaphisek Road Dindaeng, Bangkok 10320, Thailand

Yamaha Electronics Manufacturing (M) Sdn. Bhd.
Plot #7, Kinta FTZ Jalan Kuala Kangsar, 31200 Chemor Perak Dauul Ridzuan Malaysia

Australia
Yamaha Music Australia Pty. Ltd.
17-33 Market Street
South Melbourne
Victoria 3205
Australia

Yamaha North America
Yamaha Corporation of America/
Yamaha Exporting, Inc./
Yamaha Electronics Corporation, USA
6600 Orangethorpe Ave.,
Buena Park
California 90620, USA

Yamaha Systems Technology, Inc.
100 Century Center Court, Suite 800
San Jose, CA 95112, USA

New York R&D for Wind Instruments/
Artist Services
111 8th Avenue, Suite 1531 New York, NY 10011, USA

Yamaha Music Mfg., Inc.
Box 1237-100 Yamaha Park, Thomaston. Georgia 30286, USA

Yamaha Musical Products Inc.
3445 East Paris S.E., P.O. Box 899
Grand Rapids, Mich. 49512-0899, USA

Yamaha Canada Music Ltd.
135 Milner Ave., Scarborough Ontario, M1S 3R1, Canada

Yamaha South America
Yamaha de Mexico S.A. de C.V.
Calz. Javier Rojo Gomez #1149 Colonia Guadalupe Del Moral C.P. 09300 Mexico, D.F., Mexico

Yamaha de Panama S.A.
Urbanizacion Marbell
Calle 47 y Aquilino de la Guardia
Torre Banco General, Piso No. 7 Panama, Republica de Panama

Yamaha Musical do Brasil Ltda.
Av. Reboucas 2636
Cep. 05402-Pinheiros-Sao Paulo-sp Brasil

Yamaha Music Argentina S.A.
Viamonte 1145 Piso 2-B
1053, Buenos Aires, Argentina

Index